FEAR

IS NEVER OUR FRIEND

ELIMINATING THE DESTRUCTIVE POWER OF FEAR FROM OUR LIVES

FEAR

IS NEVER OUR FRIEND

ELIMINATING THE DESTRUCTIVE POWER OF FEAR FROM OUR LIVES

GARY L. RICHARDSON

HENSLEY
PUBLISHING

Fear Is Never Our Friend

ISBN 10: 1-56322-107-1

ISBN 13: 978-156322-1071

ABOUT PHOTOCOPYING THIS BOOK

DEDICATION

This book is lovingly and gratefully
dedicated to
"The White-Shirt Man,"
my dad and hero, W. R. (Bill) Richardson

My wonderful dad, with only a third grade education, truly rose like a champion above the obvious weights that were placed upon him by birth to the place where God chose to put him. He started out in the womb of a mother who was living smack dab in the middle of alcoholism, severe poverty, a serious lack of education, and worse — no motivation to change. Both of his brothers became alcoholics. Yet, when I once asked my father why he was so different from the rest of his family, he replied that he really didn't know. All W. R. (Bill) Richardson knew was that when he went to town and saw men wearing white shirts, he decided that he wanted to be "a white-shirt man."

If ever there was a man who appeared to have the right to live in fear, despair, and hopelessness, it was my father. Although all of the excuses to maintain the status quo were available to him, my dad never gave in to any of them. I saw him face fearful situations — looking fear right square in the eye — but I never saw him give in.

In 1973, my dad came to me, asking my opinion about whether or not he should accept the pastoral position of a small church. Dad had never been a pastor before, and I knew that he had also been seeking the advice of respected church leaders. Sensing his hesitancy about accepting the position, I asked him why. He said he was concerned about his lack of education. Although he was good looking, had a great personality, and loved people, he was very conscious of his limitations.

I was surprised by Dad's response because he had never before allowed his limitations to hold him back. "Righteous indignation" rose up in me, and I told him what I was sure he already knew. I pointed out that if he believed God was calling him to this church but allowed his limitations to stand in his way, he would be seriously compromising his testimony of faith.

True to form, my dad once again looked fear in the face and, in essence, said, "You are not my friend," by accepting the pastoral position. He rose to the challenge and became God's "White-Shirt Man," sharing his fearless faith in the churches he pastored for the remainder of his life.

ACKNOWLEDGMENTS

My deepest thanks…

To my wonderful father, W. R. (Bill) Richardson, who taught me by example that fear is never my friend.

To my three children, Chuck, Chad, and Chandra, who have lovingly placed confidence in me, their father, as I launch into new territory, such as writing this, my first book.

To my friend, Pastor Wade Burleson, whose teaching and writing have been such an inspiration and encouragement to me in writing this, my first published book.

To Neal Hensley and Terri Kalfas at Hensley Publishing, for their tireless efforts and continued support for me and my message.

To all the people who, by attempting to bring fear into my life, presented many opportunities for me to put into practice my strong convictions about fear and how to overcome it.

PREFACE

W hen I was about 15 years old, a boy I didn't know, called me and threatened to "cut my guts out" because I had gone out with a girl who attended my church — a girl he considered his girlfriend.

I checked around and learned that Jimmy, who lived in another town, was larger than me, older by a couple of years, and obviously meaner than me, having been in reform school a couple of times and reportedly now running with a gang.

I made sure that he and I never crossed paths. I even took steps to hide from him.

One Saturday night when a friend brought me home from town, he told my dad how we had run from Jimmy in my friend's car and lost him. My dad put me in the car and set out to find Jimmy, saying to me in a tone he only used when he was very serious, "No son of mine will ever be a coward."

He then assured me that he would make certain that it would be a clean fight.

You see, even though my dad had given his life to Christ after meeting my mother, he and his two brothers had grown up in a non-Christian family; and as the stories went, no one messed with the Richardson boys. I had heard all their stories and understood where my dad was coming from.

Thankfully, we didn't find Jimmy. So, Dad told me that

he would give me the opportunity to settle the matter myself, but that if I didn't, he would once again get involved.

I loved and admired my father. Because I would have literally taken a beating of major proportion before I would have disappointed him, I called Jimmy and made arrangements to meet with him on a Saturday night to settle our situation.

I took my cousin with me because I knew Jimmy would have his running mates with him.

Jimmy didn't show up — which taught me another lesson. All bullies are cowards.

I had been willing to get beaten to a pulp and maybe even experience serious harm because of my dedication, love, admiration and desire not to disappoint my earthly father.

It wasn't until after I had completed the first draft of this book, and spoken to church groups several times that I realized that my father's words — "No son of mine will ever be a coward." — had planted a seed in me that caused me to be driven to become fearless.

And I did become known as being fearless — to the point that when a television show honored me as Oklahoma's Legal Top Gun my consultant, Jim Burgund, said in an interview, "The thing that separates Gary from all the other lawyers is that Gary is fearless."

Over the course of my life I have learned without a doubt that in our relationship with our Heavenly Father, if only we will come to that same place of dedication, love, admiration and desire to honor Him, then we will be fearless in all areas of our lives. But we must come to know Him for who He is in our lives. In this book you will learn this, as well as come to other understandings that will truly free you from fear.

No child of God should *ever* be a coward.

When I teach seminars to Christians, I always start by saying, "In looking back over your life how many of you can honestly say, 'Yes Gary, I can think of at least one, maybe more times when I feel that fear was an asset, a friend in a given situation'? Please raise your hands."

So far 100% of those present have raised their hands.

Because these people are typically Christians, I then ask, "Assuming that most of you are praying people — and all of us are at some time when faced with difficulty — how many of you would say that you have ever prayed for fear, or for more fear? Would *you* raise your hands."

To date, 0% have raised their hands.

Finally, I tell them, "Well, we have set the boundaries, have we not? If fear has been a friend in your life, even if only one time, why wouldn't you pray for fear? Don't we pray for the things that are beneficial to our lives?"

Scripture is replete with God's admonitions about the destruction caused by fear. Yet, the church never talks about fear as being *sin*.

It is my belief that fear is the "base" sin...that fear drives all the other sins. Fear of being lonely can cause illicit affairs; fear of not having enough can cause stealing, lying, fraud, dishonesty. We could go on and on. It is an epidemic that, for whatever reason, is not being addressed by the church.

Yet once we really understand that God is our protector/shield, and nothing can happen to us unless He causes it or allows it, we can be set free from the mistaken notion that fear of any kind is good.

If we can come to see some of the truths about God that help us in times of despair, it will greatly benefit our lives. For example, God *does* love us more than we love ourselves.

Remind yourself of that when trouble comes. He really does love you. God wants the best for us — even more than we want it ourselves. He really does. And when tough times come and bring despair, we can *know* that at that moment/time in our lives *that is best,* or else our God who loves us above all, would never allow it into our lives…*Never.*

But of course, to really accept this, we have to first recognize that God is our *protector.* This is an *absolute.* He is *all-powerful,* and my friend, that means Satan can't touch us, cannot get past God and touch us, without God allowing it. To think otherwise is to give Satan more power than God. We can see this when we truly *know* that God is all powerful and is our protector, and that the Scriptures verify both. That's why we must study God's Word, to really see who God is in our lives.

My objective in writing this book is to help you see fear much like you would a big Texas cockroach sitting on your kitchen counter.

It has no value. None at all.

My objective is also to get you to think. Either see what I am saying and say, "Yes, Gary! I now see this and agree… Fear is never my friend." or say, "Gary, I see what you're saying; but I don't agree. I still believe fear is my friend...and I am going to start praying for it."

I want you either hot or cold, not neutral. Because if you are thinking, you will find truth.

And the truth is, fear is *Never* our friend.

Gary L. Richardson

CONTENTS

FOREWORD

At the height of World War II, with England facing daily bombing from the German Luftwaffe and imminent invasion by the German army, English Prime Minister Winston Churchill took to the radio airwaves to encourage his fellow Englishmen to defend their nation. In one of the most memorable speeches of the modern era, Churchill strengthened the resolve of his countrymen to resist the feared Germans with a phrase that is etched in the annals of history. With a baritone voice and in a song-like cadence Churchill, borrowing a phrase from President Franklin D. Roosevelt, declared,

"We have nothing to fear but fear itself."

Churchill succeeded in fortifying the resolve of the English people. With courage and conviction, the Brits defended their island for an additional four years against a barrage of assaults. Historians mark Churchill's speech as the moral turning point of the war.

I first heard the actual recording of Churchill's speech as a ten-year-old boy during the 30th anniversary commemoration of the actual event. Though I probably didn't understand fully the significance of "fearing fear," I soon learned experientially what Churchill and Roosevelt proposed intellectually.

I had spent many lunch periods in elementary school hiding in fear from the older, bigger, school bully who for some reason reveled in chasing me across the playground. He never caught me, but I fearfully imagined what he would do to me if he ever did.

One day, after a long discussion with one of my teachers, I decided to not run in fear, but to stand my ground. The choice to not run so shocked the bully that when he ran after me only to catch me this time, he simply smiled, said "hello," and never bothered me again. I quickly learned that the bully in my life was not this young man; it was my fear.

Thirty-five years later I am still fighting the bully named fear. As a minister for over two decades, I am in a position to see first-hand the effects of fear in the lives of people of all ages and backgrounds. Fear does not discriminate. It paralyzes everyone. It is the mother of irrational thought. It is definitely not anyone's friend.

Yet I have noticed that for people to see fear for what it is, and for them to overcome its negative influence often requires a struggle of epic proportions. Why? Too many people, including those with faith in God, operate in an environment of fear to the point that they think with fear, act in fear, live lives built on fear, and possess very little understanding on how to live by faith.

But who can blame them? The world is full of events that give birth to fear in the heart. It matters not if fear arises from global events, such as war and terrorism, or from the heart of a panicked child who hears the garage door open and realizes his drunk, abusive father has arrived home.

Fear is measured one heart at a time, independent of the corporate emotions of others.

Second Timothy 1:7 states, "God did not give us a spirit of fear." God's very name comes from the contraction of the English word *good*. The Bible also tells us that every good thing comes from God and is a gift to us.

If God does not give us fear, it can't be good.

Fear is not good for the businessman facing a crisis. Fear is not good for the student preparing for exams. Fear is not good for the person deciding his future. Fear is not good for the faithful spouse who discovers infidelity in his or her marriage. Fear is not good for the person diagnosed with disease. Fear is not good for anyone.

Fear is never our friend.

For years I searched for a practical tool to give to people who are afraid — something that could help them identify fear in their lives and assist them in overcoming its powerful, negative influence. The book you hold in your hands is the answer to my search.

With simple language, profound illustrations, and a down-home wisdom that reaches the heart of the reader, Gary Richardson helps people understand, and eventually overcome, their fears. Drawing upon a vast resource of personal experience, a wealth of knowledge on the subject through vociferous research, and most of all, a keen insight into human nature through years of study and observation, Gary has written a book that will help countless individuals.

People who know Gary understand that he lives his life without fear. Whether running for governor of Oklahoma, performing his job as a State Prosecutor as well as the United States Attorney for Oklahoma, building a nationally recognized law firm, taking on judges that display partiality during the course of a trial, bringing in award-winning verdicts, or simply making daily personal decisions, Gary is the embodiment of what it means to live by faith and not by fear.

Fear Is Never Our Friend is a book that can help you reach that point in your life where you live without fear as well. It is replete with biblical quotations, but it is as readable to the non-Christian as to the Christian. My church used *Fear Is Never Our Friend* in small group studies and the discussion times were invaluable. It is a delight to see a person move from living in fear to living by faith.

Are you at a place where you can recognize fear in your life? Are you ready to move from fear to faith?

I commend to you *Fear Is Never Our Friend.*

In His grace,

Wade Burleson
Senior Pastor
Emmanuel, Enid, Oklahoma
President
Baptist General Convention of Oklahoma
2002-2004

*There is perhaps nothing
so bad and so
dangerous in life as fear.*

— Jawaharlal Nehru

INTRODUCTION

The wise man in the storm prays to God,
not for safety from danger,
but for the deliverance from fear.
It is the storm within that endangers him,
not the storm without.

— Ralph Waldo **Emerson**

My goal in running for governor of the state of Oklahoma in 2002 was to unite Oklahomans to create a positive tomorrow for our Sooner state. I believed then, as I do today, that only a true independent thinker, unafraid to ignore powerful political interests, could break the partisan gridlock that continues to keep Oklahoma from becoming the economic player it has the potential to become on the national and international scene.

Oklahomans needed a leader who had the determination, passion, and know-how to bring Oklahoma's Republicans, Democrats, and Independents together and get Oklahoma moving toward economic recovery. Partisan politics had created a roadblock to progress for our state, and I believed it was time for a leader who knew how to blend the best of *all* parties in a way that spelled success for *all* Oklahomans.

Running the campaign required a substantial investment of not only my own money but also my time, energy, and passion. Many of my closest friends — who believed in me and my hopes for the state — were concerned about what my dream of making a difference would realistically cost me. They asked me if I *feared* losing not only the election but also the money and time away from my family and my profession — time, they pointed out, that could never be regained or replaced.

My quick and emphatic response was always that I did not fear *losing*, as defined by our society. My decision to run for governor wasn't just about winning or losing, although I certainly wanted to win. It was much more than that. I wanted the opportunity to serve the people of Oklahoma in the way I believed — and still believe today — they need to be served. I am as dedicated today as I was then to serving either as a plaintiff's attorney or as a public servant. Both positions are about fighting for the people.

My decision to run for governor was made because I had a drive to hold a position in which I could help educate the people of Oklahoma on important issues that sorely needed examination and change.

Throughout the campaign, my friends remarked — as they have consistently over the years — that they admired my commitment to never allow fear to cause me to back down from doing the things I believe in. It is partly because of their encouragement that I decided to write this book.

The other important factor in this decision was my desire to make a meaningful difference in the lives of those who read it. It is an opportunity for me to share my faith and encourage readers to do what they feel in their hearts that God has called them to do, regardless of opposition or perceived limitations. My hope is that this book will so strengthen and motivate you, the reader, that you will have "no fear" about taking whatever risks are necessary to fulfill God's purpose for your life.

Fear has reached epidemic proportions in America today. It is almost as if it is a contagious disease that is being passed on to the multitudes, rendering them weak and ineffective, and robbing them of the joy of life. But I believe we can overcome fear in our lives with a fresh infusion of faith.

Personally, I refuse to be afraid. It is not that I don't ever *feel* fear — I experience feelings of fear and anxiety just like everyone else — but I refuse to empower those feelings and give them control. I want you to understand that whenever fear tries to invade your thoughts, you have a choice — a very important choice.

In his daily devotional book *My Utmost for His Highest*, noted Christian author Oswald Chambers wrote, "If Jesus ever commanded us to do something that He was unable to equip us to accomplish, He would be a liar. And if we make our own inability a stumbling block or an excuse not to be obedient, it means that we are telling God that there is something which He has not yet taken into account."

I realize today that, long before I read this devotional, this is what I was saying to my father when he was wrestling with the call to his first full-time pastorate. I understood his concern, but even as a young man, I knew that with God's help, he was up to the challenge. It is interesting that my father — the man who had the most impact on my life with regard to overcoming fear with faith — needed someone to boost his faith at that particular time. And God used me, the beneficiary of his treasured teaching, to help my earthly father refocus on his eternal Father and make the right choice.

Fear behaves like a rabid dog. It is neither logical nor practical. It is a paralyzing force that has overtaken and destroyed far too many dreams. Its purpose is to kill that which is most valuable within each of us — our hope, our ability to love, and our potential. It brutally assaults its victims and leaves them hopeless, confused, defeated, and lacking. I have watched fear steal all that is precious from people, leaving them bankrupt in every area of their lives. I have no admiration, respect, or reverence for fear, and I hope that as you read this book, you will learn to discount and discard fear in your life.

> The highest reward for a man's toil is not what he gets for it, but what he becomes by it.
>
> — John Ruskin

Encountering a fearful situation always brings us to a crossroads that requires us to choose between two options — fear or faith. I have had the great privilege and good fortune to learn from great people, great books, and great experiences. I will be sharing with you the powerful secrets and lessons I have learned. If you truly desire to eliminate fear's destructive power from your life, you must begin by increasing your faith, which comes from knowledge. The Bible is a good place to start. Romans 10:17 NKJV tells us that "faith comes by hearing, and hearing by the word of God."

My Most Important Lesson

My education about fear began early in my life. I learned most of what I needed to know about fear from the man to whom I have dedicated this book — my childhood hero, my father.

In 1951, when I was nine years old, my family moved to a farm in deep South Texas, just outside a little town named Rio Hondo. My dad had worked at several professions to make a living for his family, including having milk cows, driving a truck, and working as an auto mechanic. Then he decided to become a sharecropper, and moved our family of four to a twenty-acre farm in Texas. He was a sharecropper before there was such a thing as crop insurance, and our family was largely dependent on the income from our cotton crop to support us. We worked hard in the fields, and when the cotton was picked, the fruit of our labors provided for us financially.

One evening when I was in my early to mid-teens, just before harvest-time, a terrible storm destroyed our cotton crop. I can still recall it as if it were yesterday — my dad and me standing on the back porch together, watching the wrath of Mother Nature as she "did her thing." Part of the time I watched in horror as the hail relentlessly beat our cotton crop to the ground. Part of the time, with my heart pounding wildly, I watched my dad's face, struggling to find some direction for my shocked emotions. I was old enough to know this was a devastating situation, with serious consequences for our family.

As Dad and I stood there watching the forces of nature destroy our only source of income for the year, he obviously sensed my great fear and realized it was almost more than I could handle. "What are we gonna do?" I asked, trying to hide the anxiety that was quickly overtaking me. Dad could sense my anguish and hear it in my voice. As he turned slowly, I looked at the man who seemed to have the strength of a grand old oak tree. Looking into his face, I noticed that his eyes seemed to be sending me a reassuring message that said, "Don't be afraid, Son. Fear is never our friend."

As I stood there contemplating this response, he tenderly rubbed his hands through my hair and said, "I think it's time for us to go to bed." From that day until now, I have never forgotten that message about fear — one of the most important lessons of my life. This display of faith and lack of fear made an indelible impression on me that has served me well in life. I hope it will do the same for you.

I have learned the significance of the Emerson quote at the beginning of this introduction. It truly is the storm within that is the most terrifying. Our thoughts and reactions always seem to frighten us the most. There are times when fear sits close to you and whispers, "I understand you."

Fear would like to convince us that it is not only our friend, but also our best friend...that it is committed to protecting us. But I am here to tell you that fear is — only and always — an imposter and a liar. Our best interests are the opposite of what fear has in mind.

I am here to share with you a great spiritual law, and that is simply this:

Fear is* never *our friend.

— Gary L. Richardson

Be sure you put your feet
in the right place,
then stand firm.

— Abraham Lincoln

CHAPTER ONE

No Can Be a Great Answer

The Everlasting No
— Thomas Carlyle

Many people live weak and powerless lives simply because they haven't learned that they have the right to decide what will be a part of their lives. Too many people allow fear to walk right in and take up residence without resistance. These are the people who would argue that saying no to fear is naïve, unrealistic, and even unwise. This insidious intruder has tricked them into believing that fear is their friend — that it is actually beneficial to them in some way. I can understand people being confused about this concept, but I totally disagree with their thinking.

As I was talking with a friend one day, she mentioned that she had heard I was writing a book, and wondered what it was about. I told her it was about fear and the fact that fear is never our friend. The look on her face told me that she didn't agree; so I asked her if she could give me an example of how she believed fear could play a positive role in her life. She carefully considered my question, and said she could. When I asked her to share a personal example with me, she said that she was extremely fearful of snakes. She went on to say she believed that if she saw a snake curled up on the floor, all set to strike and within striking distance, her fear could motivate her to seek safety. It was her opinion that her fear would be acting as a friend and protecting her. She is not alone in believing that fear is our friend.

In their book entitled *Attachments*, two psychologists, Dr. Tim Clinton and Dr. Gary Sibcy, have this to say about fear:

> Many define courage as the lack of fear. We consider the lack of fear as a sign of anything but courage. Indeed, we see fearlessness as the hallmark of someone who lacks good sense.

I asked my friend, "What do you think a ten-month-old baby crawling across the floor would do if it saw a snake curled up on the floor?" She said, "The baby would probably crawl right over to the snake." I agreed. Then I said, "So what do you have that makes your reaction different from that of the baby?"

As she stood there contemplating my question, I said, "Knowledge," to which she agreed.

This example makes my point beautifully. You see, it is knowledge that alerts or warns us of danger, not fear. At this point, fear is optional — we can choose to act out of fear or to act in faith. Either way, our choice is the result or consequence born out of knowledge, not out of fear.

On another occasion, I was visiting with a fellow lawyer who told me that he used to love to ride horses. Then he went on to say, "But today I have a fear of riding because of my bad knees." It was another opportunity for me to share my belief that it was not fear that kept him from riding, but knowledge about his physical condition and the complications that riding might cause if he chose to ride. I convinced him that knowledge and wisdom were his friends, not fear.

Knowledge is our true friend. It is wisdom — the same wisdom that God compels us to seek in His Word — that serves to protect us. Second Timothy 2:15 tells us to "study to show [ourselves] approved unto God."

When we have knowledge of something that might harm us — whether it is a snake, relationship, lawsuit, or earthquake — we have only *two choices:* fear or faith. We cannot choose both. We cannot experience fear and faith at the same time. We can have only one or the other impacting our decisions and actions.

When we face tragedy, adversity, or anything that is inconsistent with our desires — things that are out of our control — we are forced to make a choice about how we will respond. Do we respond out of fear or faith? There is no way to avoid making this choice. It is one of life's requirements. Our choice — whether faith or fear — will determine how we react. God wants us to choose faith and say *No* to fear.

> Do not be anxious about anything, but in everything, by prayer and petition, with thanksgiving, present your requests to God. And the peace of God, which transcends all understanding, will guard your hearts and your minds in Christ Jesus.
> — Philippians 4:6-7 NIV

When we come to a crossroads, and because of knowledge we feel a level of danger, we are faced with making a critical decision. Will we choose to walk a path of fear or a path of faith? The choice is ours, and God instructs us many times in His Word to *fear not!*

In fact, I am told that there are 366 "fear not" scriptures in the Bible — one for every day of the year, and an extra one for leap years! This is a good indicator of how strongly God feels about fear. He knows that He is not on our minds when we are fearful, and that obviously grieves Him. Because He knows how fear can steal our joy and even destroy our lives, He provides the "fear not" verses throughout the Old and New Testaments. Many of the verses also assure us of His presence in our lives, and remind us of His love, goodness, and faithfulness.

We can only feel free to choose to walk in faith instead of fear when we are confident that our heavenly Father cares for us, loves us, protects us, and always wants what is best for us. When we are convinced of this fact — when we believe it deeply in our hearts — it fortifies our ability to say *No* to fear and *Yes* to a life filled with peace and joy. God did not intend for our lives to be limited and constricted by forces that attempt to control and distort our lives through fear and intimidation.

> What counts is not necessarily the size of the dog in the fight — it's the size of the fight in the dog.
> — Dwight D. Eisenhower

Back in the '70s, while still a new assistant district attorney in Muskogee, I handled a case that no one else in our office wanted to touch, much less bring to trial. "A dud," "too difficult," and "a no-winner," were just a few of the more generous assessments. The real reason the case had even stayed alive for prosecution up to that point was that the victim of the crime was the uncle of our newly-elected district attorney, Julian Fite. The other prosecutors, as well as the police who had investigated the crime, believed that failure to convict under such delicate circumstances might have negative repercussions on their careers. Their choice was to "let sleeping dogs lie." Unfortunately, that wasn't the choice of the boss.

Doctor Fite, the DA's uncle, was a prominent local physician whose residence had been burglarized of thousands of dollars' worth of silverware, jewelry, and other valuables. Donald Lee Wright, the alleged perpetrator, was arrested shortly after the break-in. This guy was an interesting individual. "Unique" might be a better word to describe his many uncommon characteristics.

Wright, a man in his mid-thirties, was handsome, confident, and gregarious. He looked like a prosperous bank executive. However, to our knowledge, he had never had full-time employment. Yet he lived with his pretty blond wife and their new baby in an attractive two-story home in Tahlequah, a community twenty miles east of Muskogee. He always drove new cars and had numerous other expensive tastes. He typically traveled across the country to ply his "business," flying first class and staying in the best hotels. But his *chutzpah* was what really set him apart. When he was arrested, he was playing short-stop on the Tahlequah Police Department's softball team.

Wright was taken into custody and charged with bur-glary before Julian Fite was elected district attorney for Muskogee County. There had been little interest in pursuing Wright's prosecution at the time of the arrest because of the perceived difficulty of the case. In addition to that, the case depended largely on the testimony of Wright's nephew. The case had been passed on the docket for at least two years, but all of that changed after Fite came on the scene. The pressure he felt because of the family relationship caused the newly-elected DA to emphatically insist that the case go to trial. We soon learned that, win or lose, he wanted a trial…period.

Once someone is charged with a crime, the concept of a "speedy trial" comes into play. However, if the defendant doesn't request quick action, the matter can stay on the books for years, as this one had. For obvious reasons, crimi-nal defendants usually don't insist on going to trial and, in many instances, Father Time can be their most important ally. So it was with Wright — time was definitely on his side. He was out on bond, and perfectly satisfied with his "status quo" existence.

When Julian Fite ordered a trial for Wright, it wasn't exactly the news my fellow prosecutors and I wanted to hear. We all wondered who would get the unpleasant assignment. A day later, Fite selected his chief prosecutor, an experienced trial attorney, to handle the case. There were great sighs of relief among the rest of us in the office.

A month or two later, however, Fite changed his mind and assigned the case to me to prosecute. I had quickly established a reputation by winning a couple of tough cases. I ended up with a fourteen-case winning streak that was reported as a record for our county. Only Mr. Fite knows his reasons for reassignment of the case, but I ended up with it.

Deep down, I was both surprised and pleased. Fite's decision meant that I had arrived. His number-one man, who previously had the case, was indeed a master supervisor, and he was loyal to his boss, but I knew I had that "fire in the belly" that was necessary if Wright was to get what he deserved — which was jail. I gladly accepted the challenge. The parameters were ambiguous — the case was Fite's personal cause. We all knew that Wright was a crook, and he needed to be convicted, and I genuinely believed I could put this guy behind bars.

Wright had the proverbial "arm's length" rap sheet, with some thirty or so charges. However, even though he had been tried a few times, he had never been convicted. Most of his offenses had never gone to trial, and those that had were "worked out" without jail time. I knew that he was, at best, a thief — and a first-class one at that! — and it was time for him to do some jail time. I immediately set the case for trial.

Courage in Court

This was to be my first appearance before Judge Billy Jack Jackson (not his real name), a laid-back, country-type from a small Oklahoma town just east of Muskogee. Billy Jack, as his friends called him, was a roving judge who came to Muskogee on occasion to hold court. I had heard that he had a habit of telling attorneys how to do their business. I hoped this was just a rumor, but when I went upstairs to that small-town courtroom, I found out otherwise.

My prosecution strategy was in place, the witnesses were ready, and I walked into the courtroom full of confidence. Sam Caldwell, Donald Wright's attorney, was already seated. Caldwell was considered by many to be one of the top defense attorneys in eastern Oklahoma. As I started to sit down, Judge Jackson motioned for Caldwell and me to join him in his chambers. I was a bit puzzled by the request because to me it was an unusual way to start a trial.

Once the door closed, Judge Jackson put his hands on his hips and smiled at me. "Mr. Richardson," he began. "I've read the transcript of the preliminary hearing, and there is no way you can win this case. I've talked to Mr. Caldwell, and he has agreed to plead out Mr. Wright to a misdemeanor. I want you to reduce the charges, accept his plea, and I'm going to give him six months to a year in county jail."

For a second, I thought I must have misunderstood him. "You want me to do *what?*" I asked.

"Misdemeanor, Counselor, and that's that."

I was perplexed. I had read the same transcript. I knew the answer he wanted from me was yes. I also knew that getting a conviction was a long shot, but I wanted the opportunity to try. I believed it was wrong that the man had lived such a life of crime, and received punishment that amounted to little more than a slap on the wrist. Surely this time would be Wright's time of reckoning.

I shook my head, and said, "Judge, I'm sorry, but my answer is no. I can't do what you're asking of me. This man deserves to be convicted of a felony."

Judge Jackson squinted at me. "You don't understand, Mr. Richardson. I told you that's what I *want* you to do."

I stood my ground, and once again calmly answered, "No sir." Maybe he thought he could take advantage of me because I was a young and relatively inexperienced prosecutor, but I believed in what I was doing, and couldn't find any other answer in me but no."

With fearless resolve, I said, "I can't honor your request, Your Honor. I won't. Donald Wright has a long list of charges that he's never been convicted of. There have been a couple of trials on some of them, but he has been acquitted every time." I looked the judge in the eyes and said, "We may not win this case, but the state has the right to try it. Mr. Wright will know that he has been challenged in our county. So, respectfully, Sir, my answer must be no.

The judge was furious. Without saying anything, he headed back into the courtroom. Caldwell and I followed, and the trial began.

About thirty minutes into the proceedings, Judge Jackson began giving me bad rulings — sustaining Caldwell's objections one after another. At first, since I had never tried a case before Judge Jackson, I thought that he might have a hearing problem or, worse yet, that he didn't know the law or just didn't care about justice being done. But his one-sided decisions continued, and they were so obviously wrong that longtime observers in the courtroom coughed and squirmed. I chafed at what I came to realize were Judge Jackson's intentional acts of revenge, but I attempted to stay with my game plan.

At one point, I walked toward the chalkboard to write some pertinent information on the board to present to the jury. Mr. Caldwell objected even before I could get it written on the board. Judge Jackson quickly sustained his objection, denying me the right to make my point by following a procedure of writing on the chalkboard that is allowed time and again in the process of trying a case.

I studied the judge's face to see what I could make of this — much as I had studied my father's face as a youngster during the storm that destroyed our cotton crop. A few minutes later, I asked a question of a witness that, if answered honestly, would have been devastating to the defense. But before the witness could answer, Mr. Caldwell jumped to his feet and objected by shaking his head. Judge Jackson asked him what the grounds were, and he nervously mumbled, "It's...uh-uh-uh...repetitious, Your Honor," obviously knowing otherwise but needing something to say.

The first quality of courage is the willingness to launch with no guarantees. The second quality of courage is the ability to endure when there is no success in sight.

— Brian Tracy

"Sustained!" Judge Jackson declared, looking back at me with a smirk on his face.

I was furious. "Judge, that question has not been asked, and it has not been answered. I challenge the court to read the record. As a matter of fact," I continued, "I want it read. I'm not going to ask another question until the court goes back through the record and it's proven that the question has neither been asked nor answered." I knew I was right, but I could sense that I had crossed the line with the judge this time.

Judge Jackson sighed, called for a short recess, and instructed the jury to wait in the hall. But before they exited the courtroom, he glared at me and said loudly enough for the jury to hear, "Mr. Richardson, I want to see *you* in my chambers!" Then he smiled and lowered his voice. "Mr. Caldwell, you may join us, if you'd like."

In chambers, Judge Jackson exploded. "Richardson, I don't appreciate your conduct one whit. I won't put up with it. If you ever do anything like that again in my courtroom, I'll summon the sheriff and have you locked up so fast you won't know which direction is north!" he bellowed as he glared at me. "Do you understand me?" he demanded.

"Yes, Your Honor," I responded.

"All right, then, let's go back to the courtroom and get this case over with."

Standing Up for What Is Right

I felt compelled to make my record, regardless of what might happen to me personally. So I said, "Wait just a minute, Your Honor. I have listened carefully to what you have said, and I would appreciate it if you would extend that same courtesy to me. Otherwise, it might be a waste of time to go back to the courtroom."

I stepped toward the bench and continued, "You're upset with me because I wouldn't agree to reduce this case to a misdemeanor. I assume that you feel I have somehow shown disrespect for the court, but that was not — and is not — my intention. It is just that you don't have the authority to tell the district attorney's office how to handle its cases. It is not right for you to tell us to prosecute or not to prosecute — that is a decision we must make at our discretion. If you did have that authority, I would certainly comply with what you asked. But as long as I'm in the position of being a state prosecutor, I have an obligation to the state of Oklahoma to stand up for the rights of the people — and I must do so."

Judge Jackson glared at me as I continued, "And you have threatened me, saying if I repeated what I did in your courtroom a few minutes ago, you would have me locked up. It's obvious that you're trying to intimidate me. So you need to know that if you intend to continue giving me bad rulings — and I am now confident that you know they are bad rulings — I don't think I have the ability to contain myself. So my suggestion to you, Sir, is that you go ahead and cite me for contempt of court, call a mistrial, summon the sheriff, and have me locked up. My decision is firm. Whenever I'm in the courtroom, I'm going to do all I can possibly do to see that the state gets a fair trial. And if you intend to see that we don't, then I'm headed to jail anyway," I said.

I stopped, took a long breath, met his stare, and continued, "If I should go to jail, I only want one phone call, and it won't be to my lawyer. It will be to the newspaper."

Judge Jackson was furious, but from the look in his eyes, I knew I had captured his attention. What I was doing was right, and he knew it. He nodded curtly and motioned us back to the courtroom.

When the trial resumed, the judge completely reversed his trend of bad rulings toward the state, more consistently overruling Mr. Caldwell's objections and sustaining mine. I think he was convinced that I was willing to go to jail to ensure that the state got a fair trial — and, of course, I was!

Throughout the rest of the proceedings, Donald Wright's wife sat on the front row of the courtroom, holding their baby — an effort to reinforce the devoted family man appearance. Wright tried to maintain his composure in the courtroom. In his closing argument, Sam Caldwell took advantage of this contrived domestic scene, and told the jury, "All Mr. Richardson wants to do is to take a fine man out of his home, away from his loving wife and baby."

When it was time for my closing argument, I countered: "Ladies and gentlemen of the jury, I think Mr. Caldwell has his information mixed up. It is not about my taking anybody out of his home. Donald Wright made that decision when he broke into Dr. Fite's house. *He* made that decision. *He* decided that he was willing to be taken out of his home, away from his wife and child. *He* took that risk by stealing from innocent people. *These* are the facts for your consideration."

As I mentioned earlier, our key witness had been Wright's nephew, who had been involved in many of his uncle's capers. In an effort to avoid jail time for himself, he had cooperated with the state in the prosecution of this case. As many do, he made a deal. Caldwell had done his best to discredit the young man, but I was optimistic that if the jury believed the nephew's story, they would conclude that Donald Wright had committed the burglary.

After the jury retired to deliberate, I was standing in the hallway when Wright motioned for me to come over and join him. "Well, Mr. Richardson," he said, "I want to tell you two things. First, you don't have any business being a prosecutor. With your style of communication and fervor, you ought to be a Baptist preacher. The way you make a closing argument — all worked up and sure of yourself — you ought to be thumping a Bible and spreading the gospel."

I smiled, noting his sincerity. Then he went on. "I want to congratulate you for doing what nobody else has ever been able to do. You're going to get me convicted."

I raised my eyebrows at that statement, and responded, "Donald, it's a little early for congratulations. You never know what a jury will do."

He shook his head slowly, and said, "No, I've been in enough trials to know when I've been had. But in the unlikely event there's a hung jury, Gary, I would like for you to make a commitment to me that you won't prosecute me next time. If there is a hung jury and a retrial, let one of the other assistants handle the case."

> It is one of the most beautiful compensations of life that no man can sincerely try to help another without helping himself.
>
> — Ralph Waldo Emerson

I replied emphatically, "I can give you my commitment, but it's not the one you're asking for. I'll commit to you that as long as I'm a prosecutor in this county, and as long as you're breaking the laws in this county, I will do everything within my power to put you behind bars. You need to know that. It's nothing personal with me — but it is my job, and I will do it to the best of my ability."

Wright looked at me eye-to-eye. There seemed to be not only a look of anxiety but also a look of relief. I wondered how long he had lived his life on the edge, knowing that at some moment he would surely get pushed off.

"Donald," I continued. "If you lose and go to the penitentiary, you could use that time to make something positive out of your life. You could study great books, one of them being the Bible, and make a decision to become the person you were meant to be. This could be a real chance for you to get your life right with God and society.

"Then, when you get out, you could be a real witness to young people about getting straight and assuring them that crime never pays."

"The jury is back," a voice called out.

Wright and I went back to the courtroom, and everyone stood waiting for the foreman of the jury to read the verdict. A few seconds later, he read it aloud: "Guilty. Guilty as charged."

The punishment was set at five years in the state penitentiary at McAlester. Before Wright was led away, I leaned across the table toward him and said, "Donald, you are a for-tunate man. You could have gotten fifteen years. I encourage you to use the next five years to create a new life for you, your wife, and your child."

> As [a man] thinks in his heart, so is he.
> — **Proverbs 23:7** NKJV

District Attorney Julian Fite embraced me after the verdict. He was thrilled. "Fantastic job, Gary," he exclaimed. Then he shook my hand and thanked me again. His relief at the outcome radiated from the broad smile on his face.

I knew that he had been worried about losing the case, especially because it involved his uncle. Fite was a good man to work for. He gave me the responsibility of conducting our part of the trial; he let me do my job without interference; and we won. As a young prosecutor, I had made my boss happy, and I felt that justice had been served in the process. I was on top of the world.

After his release from prison, Wright never committed another crime in Muskogee County, as far as I know. I now believe that his burglary of Dr. Fite's home was his last offense in our jurisdiction.

I never had any further problems with Judge Jackson after the Donald Wright trial. As a matter of fact, in addition to friendly exchanges in the courtroom, he occasionally called me to his chambers to discuss issues. I know that he saw my courage and sincerity and came to respect it. I can honestly say that I have spent my career fighting for what I believe to be the best of what this country stands for.

Say No to the Negatives

There are many wrongs that we need to stand up to in our lives — many situations when it would serve us well to say no. It is certainly important to say no when it comes to filling our heads with what psychology professionals call negative self-talk. I simply call it *junk*.

Nothing is more destructive and dangerous than a life controlled by negative thinking. There is nothing "realistic" or "noble" about thinking or speaking negatively. Some people may try to convince you that they are simply "realists" who want to help you keep your feet firmly planted on the ground. They may really believe what they are telling you; but I don't buy it. I am known for confronting "realistic" people when they talk negatively. My standard response is, "Why in the world do you want to put that junk in your head? Does it make you feel good? Does it earn you money? Does it improve your life in any way? But, more importantly" — and I must confess that I most often only think but don't say — "does it bring glory to God?"

The answer, of course, is always no. And my next question is, "Then why do you do it?"

A fellow lawyer sat in my office a while back and began sharing some of the negative feelings he was having about himself that day. I proposed to him that I could come up with equally compelling evidence to support the fact that the opposite of what he was saying about himself was the truth. I could cite positive characteristics in the same areas in which he was referring to himself negatively.

He laughed and said, "You're probably right."

Then I asked him, "Why would you want to put that junk in your head when you could just as easily find evidence to support the opposite?" Of course, he didn't have a good answer — there typically isn't one — so I had given him some good food for thought.

Something that had perplexed me for many years is why negative-thinking people are so often thought of as being wise. I once had a law partner who was one of the most negative-thinking, junk-thinking people I had ever known. There were times when I thought his constant fearful and negative talk might drive me insane. And yet he had such a reputation around town as being wise. This always baffled me, until one day a psychologist friend of mine explained it, using a legal analogy.

He said, "Gary, suppose that one day a client walks into your office looking for legal advice. After he presents the facts to you and your partner, you express hope and optimism about the possibility of winning his case while your partner expresses his negative concerns. Then suppose that your firm takes the case, and even with all your hope, optimism, and hard work, loses.

"The client is very disappointed and becomes upset. Who does he blame? Of course, he blames you. You were the one who gave him hope. His natural inclination then is to think of your partner as being the wiser of the two. But your negative, fearful, and cautious law partner only *appears* to have been wise.

"But what if your firm had won the case? Who would be upset then? No one. Who would be blamed? No one. So your law partner had nothing to lose by playing it safe with his negative, pessimistic position."

Sadly, this scenario is an example of the attitude many people have in their approach to life. They think, *If I don't get my hopes up, then I won't get disappointed.* But they don't consider the price they pay when it comes to their peace, joy, happiness, health, and success in life. Happy, successful people are not negative, fearful, and anxious. By choosing to take the easy way out instead of being willing to take the necessary and priceless risks often associated with a positive, optimistic approach to life, people live far below their potential. These people rarely ever see life as experiencing, but rather, as enduring.

Some will cite examples of how fear caused people to act in a positive way to help someone in trouble, perhaps even saving someone's life. Let's explore that thought. Consider the underlying motivation for brave or heroic actions. Is fear the true motivation, or is it love that moves us to act? I will agree that in situations that call for bravery, a sense of fear has most likely been present. However, the motivation that moves a person to risk a brave act in order to help someone else is not fear but love.

Fear does not motivate us toward risk. Fear, in most instances, does just the opposite, prohibiting action. It freezes us, just as negative, fearful thoughts freeze our potential to live in the greatness God has planned for our lives.

We must remember that words are powerful. God spoke everything on this earth into existence. We are created in the image of God, and our words have power to create our realities. Words — whether positive or negative, spoken out loud or whispered to ourselves — shape our lives. God has given us free choice. It is one of the greatest of His gifts to us. Only we can choose our words and thoughts, and ultimately the path of life we choose to follow. We can use words for good or evil; to build up or destroy; to point us or others in a God-honoring direction or down a path of regret.

> *Words have
> longer life
> than deeds.*
> — **Pindar**
> **Nemean Odes IV**

Charles Dickens, in one of his well-known quotations, speaks about a fellow who was "nobody's enemy but his own." I've heard a similar saying many times during my life, which says *we are our own worst enemy*. So often that is true; but we don't have to be our worst enemy. It has never made sense to me that people would be willing to tell themselves negative things when it would be just as easy to find positive things on which to focus.

In reality, the mind can only create what we tell it.
That's why it is so important to choose with great care the
thoughts we feed our subconscious mind. If we choose to
obsess about problems, shortcomings, and lack, how can we
expect a life of positive, joyful abundance? It simply can't
happen because it goes against both universal law and spiritual law. So if you want to change your life, you must start
by changing your thinking.

How do you do that? By changing the thoughts that
you allow to fill your mind, and also by changing the words
you choose to speak, both to yourself and to others. You can
eliminate anything that you don't want simply by refusing to
dwell on it, worry over it, or obsess about it. The only way to
overcome negative thoughts is by replacing them with positive thoughts. *What you think about, you bring about.* There
are plenty of positive things to think about — you just need
to search for them.

The apostle Paul gives good advice with these words:

> Let no unwholesome word proceed from your
> mouth, but only such a word as is good for edifi-
> cation according to the need of the moment, that
> it may give grace to those who hear.

> — Ephesians 4:29 NASB

You hold the power to create your own experiences in
life. God granted you that power when He created you in
His image. Notice that I didn't say, you have the power to
control what happens in your life. The power you have is
even greater. You have the power to create how you will
respond to what happens to you. You have the power to

determine how you are going to feel and react to what happens in your life. No one can make you live your life as a victim. It is important for you to realize the power you hold in your hands. You, and you alone, choose the direction of your life. No one else has that power over you — no one. You simply have to choose to be aware of the thoughts that you allow to create your internal experience, which becomes your outward reality.

Refusing to Remain a Victim

I recently watched a television program that described the experience of a popular local news anchorwoman in a fairly large metropolitan area who had been brutally raped. Rape is a terrible and savage crime that can leave its victims marred for life. But not this woman! Although a stranger had raped her one night, she determined that she would not allow him to steal her peace, her joy, or her professional career. Instead of living in fear and ruminating about the horror of it all, she made up her mind that she would be thankful to God that the man had not killed her or left her disfigured.

She followed the admonition of 1 Peter 5:7: "Give all your worries and cares to God, for he cares about what happens to you" (NLT). She gave the terrible experience — and all the lingering fears that came with it — to God and trusted Him to take care of her. She asked Him to teach her what He wanted her to learn from the whole sordid experience. Then she laid it "at the foot of the cross" and vowed never again to allow the perpetrator to steal another moment of her life by replaying the ordeal in her mind.

Too often, we keep the pain of what we have experienced alive simply by hanging on to the memories. We allow the painful experiences to play out in our heads as if it were a movie we wanted to see more than once. Some may say, "Well, you don't understand! What happened to me was so terrible that I can't let go of the memory."

I say, "*You* are the only one who can."

Often the response will be, "But if I simply let it go, it will be as if nothing bad ever happened. I can't let the person who hurt me get off that easily." The truth is you don't have to. You can release its power over you personally, even though you should and may pursue criminal charges against the perpetrator. If you do, let the authorities handle the matter while you get on with your life. You may be called to testify, but even then you can do so without fear or the emotional trauma that is usually associated with it. By releasing the fear, anger, and guilt, you can avoid being trapped in the bondage of the experience.

God wants to relieve us of our painful memories of the past, but we must be willing to replace the negative thoughts that seek to fill our minds with wonderful thoughts of joy, happiness, and peace that come from God.

Philippians 4:8-9 gives us good advice: "Think about the things that are good and worthy of praise. Think about the things that are true and honorable and right and pure and beautiful and respected…And the God who gives peace will be with you" (NCV). When fear and unwelcome thoughts try to intrude, we can overcome them by thinking about good memories — times of joy, happiness, and peace.

We must guard the thoughts we allow in our minds and the emotions that go along with them. If we don't stop the negative thoughts, we will soon find ourselves talking negatively. "Out of the abundance of the heart the mouth speaketh" (Matthew 12:34). What we allow in our hearts and minds will eventually show up in how we talk and what we do.

Allowing negative thoughts to take up residence in our heads can be a dangerous proposition. The subconscious mind works hard to bring about the thoughts we focus on the most. The Bible verifies this: "What I always feared has happened to me " (Job 3:25 TLB).

If you allow negative and fearful thoughts to live in your mind, you will discover that they are expensive tenants. They will steal all that God has for you, taking up space that He wants to fill with thoughts of faith. So when you start to worry and feel anxious or fearful, you must immediately evict those thoughts and feelings, and take faith as the tenant of your mind instead of fear.

Instead of obsessing over something bad that *might* happen, begin to think about all the wonderful blessings God has given you to enjoy. Fear and worry will lose their power over your life if you will stop allowing them to live in your head.

Ask yourself the question I so often ask, "Why in the world would you want to put that junk in your head?" It only brings you distress, fear, and anxiety, so stop the negative thoughts with hopeful, faith-filled thoughts.

Some may think this is foolish…or that it is more difficult than I realize. You may think that I don't understand how difficult it is to change the way you have always thought, especially with regard to fear. For those who are struggling with giving up your fear cold turkey, here is a strategy that can help you kick the fear habit:

1. Imagine the best possible outcome for your given situation, or remember one of your happiest memories.

2. Then, for a quick moment, allow yourself to think of the worst thing that could happen in a particular situation you are concerned about. Take a couple of cleansing breaths, slowly breathing in through your nose and out through your mouth. Then ask yourself if you can live through the worst-case scenario. If you can, there is nothing to fear, and you can immediately go back to number one. If you don't believe you can handle the worst thing you can think of, try number three.

3. Remember God, and put Him first. Matthew 6:33 tells us that when we put God first, He will supply all our other needs. Ask yourself, *"Does God know what is best for my life?"* Do you believe that He has a plan for your life that is greater than the one you may have for yourself? Do you trust God with the life He has given you? If the answers are yes, go back to number one; if you are still not sure, go to number four.

4. Consider what you are afraid of. Are you afraid that you may lose something, or that you may not get something that you have your heart set on? Again, take a couple of deep breaths and allow your body to relax for a moment. Now it is time for some reflection. Look back over your life and examine your struggles. How have they impacted you? We often consider

only the ways our struggles have impacted us negatively. But I would like for you now to reflect on any positives that have been borne out of your trials. Have you grown from them? Are you stronger because of them? What have they taught you? Can you see God's hand in any part of them? Do you believe that He can use these experiences for *your* ultimate benefit and for *His* glory?

Once you have given yourself adequate time to reflect on these questions, write on a piece of paper all the ways that you have grown from your past experiences. Write down the ways in which they might have made you stronger, wiser, more competent, courageous, patient, faithful, humble, or appreciative. Once you have really evaluated the positives that have come from your past struggles — and I know you will find many — ask yourself if you believe that God is a loving God who has a great plan for your life. If the answer is yes, go back to number one, but if you are still afraid, go back to number one and start the process over again until you are no longer allowing fear to dominate your mind.

Flexing your faith muscle is like strengthening any other muscle in your body — it takes work. The more we use a muscle, the stronger it becomes. The more you challenge yourself to choose faith instead of letting fear grip and twist your heart, the more peace and happiness you will experience in your life.

The Advantages of Saying No

It is one thing to tell someone else no, but it is an entirely different experience to have someone say no to us. It is easy to listen to those who agree with us and say yes. Typically we are looking for a yes answer when we ask most questions; but some of our best information and learning experiences come from receiving a no answer. If we will calm our egos and control our desire to manipulate and dominate our outcomes, we can discover that being told no can be far more valuable and enlightening than always being told yes.

If we are willing to listen carefully to those who disagree with us, we have an opportunity to discover weak areas of understanding and strengthen them. Show me where someone's strength is, and I'll show you where their potential weakness is. Our great strengths and weaknesses are like sisters that go everywhere hand-in-hand. It always feels good to have someone agree with us and tell us yes. It feels good to receive a compliment or a positive word of encouragement. Yet it can be equally valuable, or even more so, to receive a no…or to receive constructive criticism about one of our actions or ideas.

> Try not to become a man of success but rather try to become a man of value.
>
> — Albert Einstein

We all know how great it feels when we get the answer we desire, especially with efforts that come easily and naturally. But it can be even more valuable when we come up against difficult and complicated challenges and work our way through them.

Through adversity, we are introduced to ourselves. Whatever comes — a yes or a no — there's something to be gained from it. Whether it is what we wanted or planned for or not, there is always important and useful information we can gain. There is always a silver lining in sharing differences of opinions, because these differences allow us to stretch and expand our awareness of ourselves and the world. The more we gain confidence and comfort from this idea, the more we will be able to welcome differences of opinion. If we will stop reacting defensively, it won't be long until we actually realize that no can be a great answer — one that can be used to our benefit.

Adversity Has a Beautiful Way Of
Introducing Us to Ourselves

QUESTIONS FOR REFLECTION & DISCUSSION

1. Can fear play a positive role in someone's life?
2. Give an example of a way you have always thought of fear as being a positive in your life.
3. When faced with something that may harm us, what two choices do we have?
4. Is fear a choice we make? If so, from where does it come?
5. All of us, at some time, face tragedy or adversity in life. When this happens, we are forced to decide how we will respond: with fear or with faith. To choose fear means that we intend to handle the circumstance on our own. To choose faith means we are confident that our Heavenly Father will guide us through it.
    - Identify the consequences of responding with fear.
    - What are the results of responding with faith?
6. We all know someone who habitually thinks or responds in a negative manner. What does negative thinking have to do with fear?
7. Second Timothy 1:7 tells us "God hath not given us the spirit of fear; but of power, and of love, and of a sound mind."
    - Have you experienced a time when God replaced your fear with his power?
    - In what ways can love replace fear?
8. What does a sound mind (some translations say *self-control*) have to do with fear?
9. You may know someone who says that fear caused him or her to act in a positive manner: by doing a heroic deed, etc. Was the underlying motivation fear, or love?
10. Does fear motivate us toward risk? Who can forget the image of a young Chinese man defying the entire Chinese military in Tiananmen Square, Beijing? He stood alone in front of a column of tanks, effectively halting their progress, after the massacre of pro-democracy protesters in 1989. Was he motivated by fear? If not fear, then what was his motivation?

11. "God said, 'Let there be light: and there was light' " (Genesis 1:3). Words are powerful. God spoke the universe into being. We have the power with our words to shape our lives and the lives of others, whether in a positive way or a negative way.
    - What are some ways we speak negatively to ourselves?
    - What are some ways we can positively impact the lives of those around us by the words we use?
    - How can we change the thoughts that fill our minds?

12. In Ephesians 4:29 the apostle Paul wrote, "Let no unwholesome word proceed from your mouth, but only such a word as is good for edification according to the need of the moment, so that it will give grace to those who hear."
    - Paul indicated that we have the power to control what thoughts we allow ourselves and what words we choose to speak. List some specific circumstances in which we can choose to think in a positive manner when we may be tempted to think negatively: How can guarding our thoughts change our personal reality?

13. What is the biggest problem with allowing yourself to think negatively, or allowing your mind to obsess and worry over something you fear?

14. "It is through adversity that we are introduced to ourselves."
    - Do you agree with the above statement? Why or why not?
    - If you agree, how does one come to know oneself through adversity?
    - If you disagree, what are your reasons?

POINTS FOR REVIEW
  ▶ Fear is not a positive thing, but it is a choice we make.
  ▶ Words are powerful. We have the power with our words to shape our lives and the lives of others.
  ▶ It is through adversity that we are introduced to ourselves.

*Make a strong and permanent commitment
to invest your talents only in pursuits
that deserve your best efforts.*

— Nido Quebein

CHAPTER TWO

Options Are Overrated

You have brains in your head.
You have feet in your shoes.
You can steer yourself
any direction you choose.

— Dr. Seuss
Oh, the Places You'll Go!

F or all of your life, you probably have been encouraged to consider *all* of your options. You may have been told that having many options is a good and positive thing. But it has been my experience that having too many options can result in confusion and a lack of direction. All successful people will tell you that most of their favorable outcomes were a result of their ability to focus. But focus in and of itself is not enough — you must learn to focus on the *right* thing, which is the purpose of God for your life. This concept follows the laws of physics, which tell us that two entities cannot occupy the same space at the same time.

This is certainly true of fear and faith — they cannot operate simultaneously in the same space. Faith does not operate on feelings, but fear feeds and thrives on feelings. Fear looks inward and finds instability. Faith looks toward

God to find security and stability. The best way to deal with your fears is to have a fixed focus of faith on the person of Jesus Christ. But the decision is yours; you can only choose to be faithful to one, and you are the one who must do the choosing.

As Dr. Seuss so simply put it, "You have brains in your head. You have feet in your shoes. You can steer yourself any direction you *choose.*" The key word in this statement is choose. You must choose the direction you want to go…and then go for it!

Life offers us many opportunities for making choices, and most of them involve choosing what is right or wrong. All of these choices are critical to our overall well-being. I experienced such an opportunity when I found myself in a court trial that was to determine how the assets of a law firm should be divided between a former partner, a current partner, and me.

It's as Simple as Right or Wrong

During the trial, an issue arose that, if the truth were told, would cost my partner an additional $82,000 and me an additional $270,000. Our attorney urged us not to disclose this information because it was the opposing side's fault for not discovering this information during the discovery period preceding the trial. My partner and I disagreed with him because we both believed that we had only one "right" option — to do the right thing. We didn't want money that wasn't ours. We expressed our belief that not revealing the truth in this situation would be as wrong as robbing a bank.

We chose the direction that we knew was right — and we never looked back. We shared the information with the opposing side, and gave up the money that rightfully belonged to our former partner. Why were we able to do that? Because we knew about the peace that comes with doing the right thing — acting with integrity. To me, that peace is worth far more than silver and gold.

People of honesty and integrity believe in wholeness, goodness, excellence, and truth, and they are good examples for others. Such respected people are not willing to compromise their values.

Many in our world today, however, would find it extremely difficult, if not impossible, to make such a decision. Fear of losing what they think they need — or of not having enough — can cause people to make decisions that continue to cost them far into the future. Losing one's integrity is a high price to pay, because when we sell our integrity, we have very little left.

A life lived with integrity — even if it lacks the trappings of fame and fortune — is a shining star in whose light others may follow for years to come.

— Denis Waitley

When our eyes are focused on truth and what is right, we recognize that many of the options offered to us by the world are sorely overrated. When we are focused on what is right, we seem to have an almost automatic ability to make right choices. We don't have to fear not having enough, because we know that God knows our needs better than we do. We don't have to fear not having enough, because we know that God is an abundant and generous God, and He will always provide the right amount of everything we need in our lives. He made us that promise in His Word.

Jesus himself gives us this great assurance in Matthew 6:25-26: "Don't worry about everyday life — whether you have enough food, drink, and clothes. Doesn't life consist of more than food and clothing? Look at the birds. They don't need to plant or harvest or put food in barns because your heavenly Father feeds them. And you are far more valuable to Him than they are" (NLT). Knowing that God cares for us infinitely more than the birds should convince us of the wisdom of choosing faith over fear.

> We should every night call ourselves to an account: What infirmity have I mastered today? What passions opposed? What temptation resisted? What virtue acquired?
>
> — Marcus Annaeus Seneca

When fear encourages us to make decisions that are not in agreement with what God says is best for our lives, we must remember that He knows best. If we make wrong choices out of fear, we are leaving God out of the formula, which means we won't get the best results. It is always in our best interest to follow God's plan. Even though the right choice may be difficult, God assures us that He will never leave us nor forsake us. (See Hebrews 13:5.) He is always there to encourage and strengthen us and help us make choices that will bring Him glory and make our lives better.

After our trial was over, a friend asked me why I had made the decision to disclose the truth regarding the money and releasing it to my former partner. He wondered if my former partner would have done the same for me had the shoe been on the other foot. "There is no way to know for sure," I explained. "What my former partner might choose to do or not to do is his business. But what I choose to do defines who I am." I knew that by making the right decision, I had kept God in the formula for my life and brought Him glory — and that is the only option that matters.

When our mind races, with many ideas or options continually bouncing around, it is sidetracked with distractions. Our mind can become so busy contemplating all the optional directions that it ends up going nowhere. But when our mind chooses one option — the right option — on which to focus its attention, it gets to work making that option a reality in the physical world, by directing our actions. Focus begins with desire, and out of our desire, our priorities are born.

What do you truly desire?

We are created in God's image for relationship with Him. Our greatest desire should be to know God and to have a relationship with Him. That is how we are designed, and until we have that relationship with our Creator we will never be truly satisfied with anything else. Psalm 37:4 NIV says, "Delight yourself in the Lord, and he will give you the desires of your heart." Only God can satisfy the desires of every human heart for joy and peace, which are most likely at the top of everyone's priority list.

It is important then, to consciously and continuously fill your mind with thoughts of God's goodness, seeking His direction for your life. Your thoughts are extremely important. They determine the direction you will go and empower that about which you passionately think. If you want to change things in your life, you must create an internal shift. You must shift your way of thinking so it is consistent with the outcome you desire. Along with this shift in your think-ing, you must act in ways that are consistent with your new thoughts. If you want something different, you must *do* something dif-ferent in order to get it. Having too many options will distract you, causing you to waste your precious time and energy on things that ultimately will not take you where you want to go. There is only one direction for those who believe in God's holy sanctity, and that direction is always the one that leads us closer to Him. We must always move confidently and coura-geously toward truth and trusting God regardless of the cost. We must long to be more like Him, and to bring Him glory in everything we do.

> *Fear is merely creative thought in negative form.*
>
> — **Robert Collier**
> **The Secret of the Ages**

Consider how omitting your most familiar negative options might impact your life. For example, how would your life be different if you eliminated the option of giving in to your fear? Most of you have grown accustomed to your fear...you are familiar with it. How would your life be dif-ferent if, instead, you grew accustomed to believing that you could trust God with every need in your life? What if you realized that fear is never your friend and eliminated it as an option? Unfortunately, most people cannot go so far as to even *imagine* their lives without fear.

David R. Hawkins, M.D., Ph.D., in his book *Power vs. Force*, a study that was in process for twenty years on the subject of kinesiology, says:

> Fear runs much of the world, spurring on endless activity. Fear of enemies, fear of old age or death, fear of rejection and a multitude of social fears are basic motivators in most people's lives. Fear is the favored official tool for control by oppressive totalitarian agencies, and insecurity is the stock-in-trade of major manipulators of the marketplace. The media and advertising play to fear to increase "market share."

He goes on to say that:

> ...the proliferation of fears is as limitless as the human imagination; once fear is one's focus, the endless fearful events of the world feed it. Fear becomes obsessive and may take any form. Fear of loss of relationship leads to jealousy and a chronically high stress level. Fearful thinking can balloon into paranoia or generate neurotic defensive structures and, because it is contagious, become a dominant social trend.

He concludes by saying,

> Fear limits growth of the personality and leads to inhabitation, and because it takes energy to rise above fear, the oppressed are unable to reach a higher level unaided.

It is Dr. Hawkins' conclusion that the fearful seek strong leaders who appear to have conquered their fear to lead them out of its slavery.

In considering the many options that are available in our lives, it would serve us well to completely eliminate fear. Frustration and uncontrolled anger, for example, are terrible options because they bring with them such misery. Choosing the negative options offered to you by the world can steal your hope of achieving the dreams that fill your heart. The only options you should consider viable are the options that lead you to your final destination — closer to God. You should choose only the options that will make you the man or woman that you believe God wants you to be. The best option is always to choose truth and right, and to keep God in the formula of your life.

It is challenging enough to eliminate options that you know negatively influence and impact your life, but how do you choose between two options that both appear to be positive and good? Many times in life, you may find yourself in situations where you must choose between two options that each have merit. The following story is a perfect example of a man who was faced with such a challenge — a man faced with two very positive options.

Making a High-Priority Choice

Steve Goodier tells the following true story of a genuine American hero in his book, *A Life That Makes a Difference*.

When the sport of canoe racing was added to the list of international competitions at the 1924 Olympic Games in Paris, Bill Havens was a member of the United States team, which was favored to win the event.

There were no jet airliners in 1924 from Paris to the United States; only slow ocean-going ships. As the opening of the Olympics drew near, Bill found himself facing a serious dilemma. The doctor estimated that his wife would give birth to their first child about the time the U.S. team was scheduled to compete in the Paris games. Should he go to Paris and risk not being at his wife's side when their baby was born? Or should he withdraw from the team?

Bill's wife encouraged him to go to Paris. She understood that competing in the Olympics was the culmination of many hours of hard work and a lifelong dream. Torn between two of the most monumental experiences of his life, Bill struggled about what he should do. But after much soul-searching, he chose to follow his heart. He decided to withdraw from the competition and stay home, where he could be with his wife and support her when their child arrived. After searching his heart, he realized that being at her side was his highest priority, even higher than going to Paris to fulfill his dream.

> When we learn to say a deep, passionate yes to the things that really matter, then peace begins to settle onto our lives like golden sunlight sifting to a forest floor.
>
> — **Thomas Kinkade**

The excitement was tremendous when the United States' four-man canoe team won the gold medal in Paris. Bill's wife's delivery was late — in fact, so late that he could have competed in the event and returned home in time to be with her for the birth. People said, "What a shame." But Bill had no regrets. He had chosen what was most important to him, what he had felt led in his heart to choose. It was difficult, but for the rest of his life, he believed that his decision — the right decision, one of selflessness — had been the best decision.

Not everyone has the strength of character to say no to something that he or she truly wants in order to say yes to something that truly matters. But for Bill, it was the only way to find peace. Many times throughout our lives, God calls on us to make these kinds of decisions. He sometimes asks us to choose between what we want and what we know in our heart is the right thing to do. Sometimes God calls us — like Abraham — to kill what we desire in order to be obedient to Him. And in proving our faithfulness, He gives us our greatest desires. (See Genesis 22:16-17 NLT.)

Such was the case for Bill Havens. The child that Bill chose over his opportunity to compete for a medal at the Olympics was a boy. Bill and his wife named him Frank. Twenty-eight years later, in 1952, Bill received a cablegram from Frank. It was sent from Helsinki, Finland, where the 1952 Olympics were being held. The cablegram read: "Dad, I won. I'm bringing home the gold medal you lost while waiting for me to be born."

Bill had sacrificed his opportunity to win a medal, choosing instead to fulfill the more important responsibility of a husband and father, and many years later, God granted Bill his medal through his son. Frank Havens and the U.S. team won the gold medal in the canoe racing event, the event and medal his father had dreamed of winning.

If you are to realize your dreams and desires, you must recognize the powerful impact of negative options and learn the importance of making right choices. There are a few that you must — yes, I said *must* — eliminate, if you are to have the success, happiness, and peace of mind that God intends for your life. One of the options that you must eliminate is speaking negatively to yourself. *You can't put junk in your head.* What you say to yourself, whether it comes out of your mouth or stays inside your head, has more power than you realize.

The Power of Thoughts and Words

The power of the mind is amazing. Our thoughts — both positive and negative — have the ability to affect our health, moods, relationships, and every other aspect of our lives. Our thinking patterns can, and do, produce many of our problems and directly affect our words and actions.

In her book, *In Pursuit of Peace*, Joyce Meyer says:
The average person has about fifty thousand thoughts a day, and for many, these thoughts are mainly pessimistic and negative. When you are confronted with a negative thought, you have the option of either ignoring it or inviting it in and analyzing and meditating on it....When you do the latter, you begin to speak out the problem with your mouth, and it becomes a word. You ponder it more, and it becomes an action. You then analyze and meditate on it more, and it becomes a habit, and unfortunately for the majority of Christians, most of their problems are simply negative thoughts that have become habits.

Joyce continues with a solution:
The Word of God admonishes us to think about things above, not things on the earth. This does not mean to sit and think about heaven all day, but it does mean to think about what God would think about.

He thinks of high things, not low things; good things, not bad things. We can think about anything we choose to, but we must remember that we reap what we sow. Thoughts are definitely seeds that will always produce a harvest in our life.

In Colossians 3:1 the Word tells us we are to "aim at and seek the [rich eternal treasures] that are above, where Christ is, seated at the right hand of God" (AMP). When we do this, we will indeed be raised with Christ to a new way of living. Verse 2 says to "set your minds and keep them set on what is above (the higher things), not on the things that are on the earth." This clearly means that we seek whatever we think about. Whatever we fill our minds with is what we are looking for, desiring, and will more than likely end up with. Remember, where the mind goes, the man follows.

It is, then, very important to control the thoughts that we allow in our minds, because the mind is the leader or forerunner of all actions.

I Am Weak...I Am Strong

Researchers once conducted a study in which they asked participants to choose between two sentences: *"I am weak"* or *"I am strong."* Then they were asked to repeat the chosen sentence silently to themselves while standing with their arms outstretched in front of them at shoulder height. In each case, the chosen sentence dramatically impacted the participant's level of strength. When the researchers conducted strength tests by pressing the arms of the subjects down toward the floor, those who were telling themselves they were strong had much greater strength to resist than those who said they were weak. In short, the people who told themselves they were strong not only *felt* strong, they actually were strong. Those who told themselves they were weak found it extremely difficult, if not impossible, to keep their arms outstretched.

So it is with the words we tell ourselves with regard to God. When we tell ourselves that He is strong — that He can and will keep His promises to us, and that we can "be anxious for nothing" (Philippians 4:6) — it has a positive influence on our lives. We begin to make better choices as a result of strengthening our hearts and minds with careful and deliberate thoughts and words.

I am always amazed when godly people buy into Satan's lie that we cannot rid our lives of anxiety. Why would a loving God admonish us to "be anxious for nothing" if it was impossible to do? He wouldn't — and didn't. We can choose to have lives that are free of anxiety by carefully choosing positive, faith-filled words.

The words we speak have a power all their own — the power to create and the power to destroy. Proverbs 18:21 NIV reminds us that "the tongue has the power of life and death, and those who love it will eat its fruit." You see, we all create and destroy every single day with the words we choose to say. Still not convinced of the power of words? Read the following paragraph:

> The early morning sun pulled at the woolen blanket of darkness that covered the sleepy village below. The cottages, surrounded by fields still glistening with the night's frozen dew, were laid out in neat rows each

with wisps of smoke climbing through dawn's sky from
warming hearths just now brought to life. The new day
was just beginning and all things were possible.

The village described above didn't exist in your mind
until you read the words. The village in the valley was "created" in your mind without television or pictures or special
effects of any kind, but now it is alive in your imagination...
using only words. That's how strong words can be, and are.
The exciting thing is that positive words are powerful too.
Try them.

Genesis 1:2-3 says "the earth was formless and empty,
darkness was over the surface of the deep, and the Spirit of
God was hovering over the waters. And God said, 'Let there
be light,' and there was light." As you know, God went on,
over the next six days to create the whole earth using only
the words from His mouth. This is God's demonstration of
the power of the spoken word — a great lesson for all of us
about the importance of the words we speak.

Words can also tear down and destroy. A simple word
heard first thing in the morning can set your course for the
rest of the day. With a positive word, you feel up, energized
and confident. A negative word can render you gloomy, sad
or depressed, fearful, and unsure of yourself. The words you
speak to others — or to yourself — either build up or tear
down. That's the power you possess in your mouth. Once
you understand this concept, you can see how important it is
to monitor what you think and say, and stop putting junk
into your head.

It is crucially important to carefully choose the words
you speak to yourself and to visualize the outcomes you

desire. If you choose to allow negative or fearful thoughts, words, and images to fill your mind, you can, and will, actually bring about what you do not really want. Like Job, you may have to say, "What I always feared has happened to me. What I dreaded has come to me" (Job 3:25 NLT).

Why would people choose to entertain negative thoughts and speak negative words, knowing the adverse impact they will have on their lives? Because of fear. They are afraid of believing something good and being disappointed — or worse, even risking losing their faith.

Choose Faith and Love

Sometimes in relationships, as in life, we must decide whether we will love or be angry. Love, like fear and faith, is a choice. We can choose faith — and the love, peace, happiness, and joy that comes with it — or we can choose fear, frustration, anger, and conflict. God has told us which of these choices originate with Him and which do not. He has given us clear directives to ensure that our lives are full of connection, love, and peace. He tells us throughout the Bible to *fear not*, and in Galatians 5:14, He says we are to "love others as we love ourselves."

> How different our lives are when we really know what is deeply important to us, and keeping that picture in mind, we manage ourselves each day to be and to do what really matters most.
>
> — Stephen Covey

We must choose faith and the love that comes with it as a gift. God asks us to choose our strong, secure, and abiding relationship with Him, as well as our strong, secure, and abiding relationships with one another. There appears to be only one good choice — and I have made that choice. I chose the love I have for Christ and the faith I have in Him.

Loving relationships bring glory to God and joy to those who experience them. Fear, and the emotions it creates inside our hearts, weakens our relationships. God intends for us, and our love, to be strong. In 1 Corinthians 13:13, He speaks of faith, hope, and love — three options — then He tells us, "the greatest of these is love" (TLB). Trust in Him. Say no to fear and yes to faith, hope, and love. Choosing any other option will cost you dearly.

In his daily devotional book, Oswald Chambers says, "Love is spontaneous, but it has to be maintained through discipline." The same is true of fear. As Christians, our faith is spontaneous, but it takes discipline to keep it alive.

Have you ever had what you believed to be an inspired idea that filled you with great joy and excitement...until fear caused you to begin to think about the "what ifs"? It is at this point that too many people choose to give up in fear instead of moving forward in faith. Because they are not diligent in maintaining their faith, they allow fear to take over their thought processes and rob them of their zeal and excitement. The end result is that they miss an opportunity to experience seeing their idea become a reality.

Choose your thoughts wisely. Monitor what enters your mind and heart — allow only those thoughts that will make you strong in your walk with God. Choose your words carefully. Speak them kindly and tenderly. Choose them for their power to bring you closer to God. Realize that you can, and do, choose your feelings every minute of every day, and that they are as easy to change as the clothes you wear.

It is within your power to make the necessary changes. One of the greatest powers God bestowed on man is the "freedom to choose." Don't confuse "freedom to choose" with "free choice." There are consequences that come with all of our choices, so they are not really "free." For example, God has given us the freedom to choose fear over faith, but what an unbelievable price we pay for that choice. As children of God, we do have the freedom to choose, but we must understand that our choices always create certain results — good or bad — depending on what we choose.

Choose faith and choose love. Choose to feel only the feelings that bless you and those you care for. Choose the feelings that bring glory to God. If you feel hateful, spiteful, angry, or frustrated, remember that you can change those feelings by simply choosing to love instead. In the process, you will discover that God and the options found in His Word are the only options you need. All others are overrated.

QUESTIONS FOR REFLECTION & DISCUSSION

1. Identify occasions when you faced adversity with fear. How did that work for you?

2. Identify occasions when you responded to adversity with peace-producing faith.

3. Discuss the differences in approaching adverse situations in fear as opposed to faith.

4. For most of your life you have probably been encouraged to consider all of your options; but when one is faced with too many options, what can be the result?

5. Probably no one would argue that the ability to focus is important, but that alone is not enough. Why?

6. The Law of Physics says two entities cannot occupy the same space at the same time. How does this relate to your focusing on the purpose of God for our life?

7. When it is necessary to make a decision about your life, which option will always bring you the most satisfaction? Why?

8. The author writes: There is a peace that comes from doing the right thing — a peace that can only be purchased with integrity. What do you think he means by this statement?

9. Why do we not need to fear losing what we think we need?

10. What do we risk when we let fear cause us to make decisions that are not in alignment with what God wants for our lives?

11. Proverbs 23:7 tells us, "as he thinketh in his heart, so is he."
   • Why is our thought life so important?
   • How might omitting your most familiar negative options impact your life?

12. How would your life be different if you eliminated the option of giving in to your fear?
   • How would your life be different if you grew, instead, accustomed to believing that you could trust God with every need in your life?
   • How does one choose between two options that both appear to be positive and good?

13. The author relates a story about Bill Havens and the choice he was forced to make between competing in the Olympics and being present at the birth of his first child. Havens chose the latter because he believed that was the best choice for him.

    • Have you ever been faced with making a difficult decision between two options, both of which seemed good?
    • How did you respond?
    • What was the result of the choice you made?

14. In the fourth chapter of Paul's letter to the Philippian Christians he wrote, "Do not be anxious about anything, but in everything, by prayer and petition, with thanksgiving, present your requests to God. And the peace of God, which transcends all understanding, will guard your hearts and your minds in Christ Jesus" (4:6-7 NIV).

    • Why are the above verses so important to us when we are faced with choosing between two options?

15. Each of us at times has had the option to love or to give in to feelings of hurt, anger, frustration, etc. How difficult is it to choose love over negative feelings?

    • If so, why do you think it is so difficult?

POINTS FOR REVIEW

  ▶ You can and do choose your thoughts, words and feelings every day.
  ▶ Choose your thoughts wisely; you become what you think.
  ▶ Love strengthens our relationships with God and others; fear weakens those relationships. Choose love.

*The dark moment the caterpillar calls
the end of the world is the sun-filled moment
the butterfly calls the beginning.*

— Unknown

CHAPTER THREE

Failure Often Is
the Beginning

Thank God for your present limitations or failure...
for you now occupy a status from which nearly all
success stories originate.

— Jim Rohn
The Seasons of Life

I f you are concerned about the possibilities of successes and failures in your life, you are not alone. Many struggle with the same concerns. We all tend to be painfully aware of our own limitations — so much so that we sometimes limit our potential. But we can't live a life of faith in some safe place. The life of faith is a life of risk, one that requires us to take action.

Laurence Shames, a writer for *The New York Times*, once wrote:

> John Milton was a failure. In writing *Paradise Lost*, his aim was to "justify the ways of God to men." Inevitably he fell short and wrote only a monumental poem. Beethoven, whose music was conceived to transcend fate, was a failure, as was Socrates, whose ambition was to make people happy by making them reasonable and

just. The surest, noblest way to fail is to set one's standards Titanically high. The flip side of that proposition also seems true.

The surest way to succeed is to keep one's striving low. Many people, by external standards, will be "successes." They will own homes, eat in better restaurants, dress well, and, in some instances, perform socially useful work. Yet fewer people are putting themselves on the line, making as much of their minds and talents as they might. Frequently, success is what people settle for when they can't think of something noble enough to be worth failing at.

Most of us have a desire to make a meaningful difference in our world and in the lives of those around us, but too often we are not quite sure how to make that happen. We know that God has a "perfect" plan for our lives, and we long to know that plan. We thoughtfully seek to define our vision and passion, but can't seem to bring it into focus.

If you have a sincere desire to know God's plan for your life, there is no need for you to worry about knowing all the specifics. Fear will keep pushing you to find all the answers, but faith and trust in God will help you to relax and enjoy the everyday experiences of life, knowing that God is in control. It is time to stop looking for God's plan for your life and instead start *living* his plan.

We worry about making a decision and taking action because we are afraid of making the wrong choice and finding out later — with the benefit of additional information — that a different choice would have served us better. Even people who have had a lot of successes say that they sometimes have a nagging feeling that they might have made a better choice.

Think about this for a minute. What kind of sense does it make to beat yourself up for decisions you made yesterday based on the information you had at that time? Today you have additional information and would make a different choice — but that isn't an option...so forget it and move on.

God can make something positive out of situations that we see as being negative. Romans 8:28 tells us that "in all things God works for the good of those who love him, who have been called according to his purpose" (NIV). God even uses your failures to bring about good.

I'll even go on record as saying that you might be surprised at how often your perceived failure is actually your friend. Look back over your life at the situations you believed to be failures — yet today you can see how the beautiful hand of God brought good from them. This should convince you not to allow the fear of failure to keep you from enjoying life.

The fear of failure blocks success in many areas of life, preventing people from living up to their God-given potentials. And what a shame, because failure is not all bad — it is not the end of the world.

In fact, I say that failure is just the beginning. Failure is nothing to fear; rather it is something we should *enthusiastically* embrace because it provides a great deal of important information.

Has anyone ever faulted a baby for falling as he or she is learning to walk? Of course not. It would be unthinkable to fault a baby for "little failures" on the road to success. So it is with God's children. We must accept that failures are a normal part of experiencing life.

Once we have experienced failure, tripped and fallen on our faces, and then picked ourselves back up, we're left with a new level of understanding — a new mastery — that is truly valuable. We have earned a degree of confidence that cannot be easily shaken. When we choose to look at failure as a beginning of something, a way to learn, grow, and develop, we will view our inevitable failure as a necessary part of the whole. Once we relinquish the anxiety about our fear of failure, we can begin to joyfully and enthusiastically focus once again on our goals.

We often fear failure because of our arrogance and pride. We think that we are somehow entitled to achieve success without paying its market price. It usually doesn't work that way. It is when we set out knowing full well that failure *is* a part of the journey — that falling short of the mark only tells us the distance left to go — that we begin to comprehend the value that each failure brings to our lives. Only then can we enjoy our life experiences to the fullest.

What we perceive as failures will always be disappointing in the beginning. They can be painful and frustrating. That's why we often think that we dislike them. But when we allow ourselves to understand that they are simply building blocks of experience — bricks in the wall of our success in walking out God's plan for our lives — we realize that with each one, we move closer to making His dreams and goals for our lives a reality. When we choose to rid ourselves of our fear of failing, we find that we are willing to risk more, do more, give more of ourselves, and be more. That is when real success is waiting for us just around the corner.

I recently read about a survey that was taken among retired people in the United States. They were asked this question: "If you had your life to live over again, what would you do differently?" Interestingly enough, the number-one answer given — by a sizable margin over the second most popular answer — was, "I would take more risks." I find that very interesting.

Let's speculate for a moment about why that was their answer. I would say that in looking back over their lives, they realized that they had not really experienced life to the fullest. They could see how fear had robbed them of the opportunity to really get out of life all that God had meant for them to have. In retrospect, they realized that they had allowed fear — the very thing their Creator had warned them against — to rob them of many beautiful life experiences.

Since you are reading this book, I can assume that you want to deal with the issue of fear and the control it has over your life. I encourage you to take the necessary steps now to rid yourself of the fear that would cause you in your old age to look back over your life and say, "I wish I had taken more risks and lived a more fulfilling life." As you examine your own life, you will realize that all your fears have been based on falsehood, a lie of Satan. You will discover that displacing the false with truth is the essence of the healing of all things, both visible and invisible.

Some say that 90 percent of the things we fear never happen. Zig Ziglar shares an acronym that also helps us look at fear in a positive way:

F alse
E vidence
A ppearing
R eal

Too many people wear fear like a badge of honor, as if it is an appropriate excuse for not facing the challenges, opportunities, and adventures life has to offer. This thought-provoking acronym should encourage you not to pass up opportunities for potential success simply because you are afraid you will fail.

In his book, *The Best of Success,* Wynn Davis tells us that the law of failure is one of the most powerful of all the success laws because you only really fail when you quit trying. When we accept the reality that failure is only the beginning of something great, we will learn to persevere.

Sharing a Dream

One of my favorite stories is about Cyrus W. Field, a man who insisted on seeing failure as a beginning. Although you may not recognize his name, he was one of the greatest entrepreneurs of the 1800s. His story began in 1853 when he gathered a small group of men at his home to share a dream. His proposal was to manufacture a communication cable that would cross the Atlantic Ocean from the New Americas to the continent of Europe. The line was to run from Nova Scotia, St. Johns, Newfoundland across the Atlantic. Cyrus believed that this cable had the potential of bringing two great worlds together, which would foster greater commerce. He even believed that his cable could possibly work toward averting the tragic kinds of miscommunication that often led to wars.

At the close of this meeting, six individuals married their sense of will to his. They agreed to attach themselves to his dream, his vision. They were not experts, oceanographers, or telegraph wire communication experts. Again, they were men who were willing to buy into Field's vision and dream.

They went to work, and five years later, in the fall of 1858, they finished laying the cable. Because of erosion difficulties caused by the salt water, the cable only worked for fragments of a message over a few seconds, and the entire effort was deemed a disaster and a hoax. It was considered to be the biggest folly of the eighteenth century.

The errors to avoid are those that eliminate opportunities to try again.

— **Lazar Goldberg**

People grew suspicious of Cyrus Field's dream. They began to doubt, and that doubt lasted for the next eight years. We know much of this story because Cyrus kept a detailed journal of the experience. This is one of Cyrus' entries: "After the failure of 1858, these became my darkest days."

It was an extremely difficult time for Cyrus. He learned what many of us have learned — that when our efforts appear to have failed, it is very difficult to raise our dreams to life again. But Cyrus was determined.

Facing Failure

Cyrus Field lived these words. For the next seven years, he and his companions pleaded with others to find a solution to the saltwater erosion. Finally, on July 15, 1865, they set sail. This time they would skip the problems of laying cable on land and lay the cable directly over the Atlantic. After 1,200 miles of cable had been laid, with only 600 miles left to go, a fault was spotted on a portion of the line. As they stopped to reel in the damaged section, a large wave lifted the boat and snapped the cable. For nine days and nights, they dragged the bottom of the ocean, searching for the sunken cable — with no success. Finally, they returned to England, defeated, yet Cyrus wrote that he was "full of resolution to start the battle anew."

Isn't it true that many men fail because they decide to quit too soon? When things start going wrong and it looks like everything is against them, they begin to lose their faith. Because they fear that the circumstances are insurmountable, they lose their courage to keep on fighting. And it is all because of how they choose to think. They choose fear instead of faith — and that really is the only way to fail.

> Success is going from failure to failure without losing enthusiasm.
> — Winston Churchill

If we would learn to step out in faith to attempt the impossible, we would quickly experience the truth of Mark 9:23 where Jesus himself says, "Everything is possible for him who believes" (NIV). By choosing faith over fear, we can accomplish anything.

One year later, after raising only enough money to replace the section of damaged cable, Cyrus and his crew sailed back out. This time they faced horrible weather conditions. They experienced dense fog, raging storms, and squalls. They felt as if they were fishing for a jewel at the bottom of the ocean. Many people believed it was not only ridiculous to try to find the lost cable but also completely impossible.

Cyrus' odd attack was simple yet gigantic. He would do his best to get to the general vicinity of the previous year's debacle, and then begin casting huge grappling hooks on the end of rope twisted with steel wire that was capable of lifting an estimated thirty tons. It took two hours for the cable to drop to the bottom of the ocean and up to thirty hours to reel it in. It was a very slow process.

On August 17, 1866, the ship's line hooked something, and twenty-eight hours later, the cable broke the surface of the sea. The crew had it in sight for almost five minutes. But, as if frightened, the cable broke away and sank once again. The crew was devastated but determined, so they lowered the hook once more.

Success At Last!

Two weeks later, they hooked something again. Forty-eight hours later, they saw their precious cable. No one uttered a single word. It was as if all life and death hung in the balance. They could hardly believe their eyes. It was only when the cable was brought onto the ship that a word was spoken. Some of the men turned their heads and wept. Some ran and celebrated with joyous screams. Thirteen years of anxious watching and ceaseless toil had finally come to a successful end. The true greatness of Cyrus W. Field was the immeasurable force of determination in his head, and the passion in his heart. He had the necessary will and knowledge to get the task done, and he refused to see failure as anything but a new beginning.

Life is an adventure. Cyrus' life took on a transcendent purpose when he refused to release the dreams of his heart. This is a good lesson for all of us. Only when we marry what is in our hearts and our minds with the courage to persevere do our dreams have a chance of becoming reality. Make the decision today that you will not allow the lies of Satan to keep you from accomplishing God's will for your life.

Try, Try Again

On a similar note, in February 2004, there was a story in the *California Bar Journal* that opened like this: "For those 3,940 lawyers who failed last July's bar exam, Maxcy Filer has some advice: Try, try, again."

Maxcy Filer took the California Bar Exam for the first time at the age of 36 in 1966, and he failed. He took it again and failed. He took it many, many more times, and each time he failed. He took it in San Diego, Los Angeles, San Francisco, Riverside, and anywhere else it was offered. Over and over, he failed.

He started taking the exam when his children were still living at home. He then took it with each of his sons as they successfully earned their own law degrees. He took it again after he started working as a law clerk in the law offices of his sons, and he continued taking it even as he reached an age when most people are seriously considering retirement.

Finally, after twenty-five years, $50,000 in exam fees and review courses, and 144 days in testing rooms, Maxcy Filer took the exam for the forty-eighth time, and passed. He was 61 years old.

Maxcy never saw each failure as the end of his dream. Instead, he saw each failure as a step toward what he believed to be the inevitable — the fulfillment of his dream.

I wonder how many of us stop one step shy of realizing our dreams because of fear. Too often, insecurity and fear — being unstable, uncertain, and lacking confidence — keep people from persistently pursuing a dream that could enrich not only their lives but also the lives of others. But that is not God's plan. Jesus tells us in John 10:10 (AMP) that "Satan comes to steal what is best for us [many times through fear]," but, He goes on to say, "I came that they may have and enjoy life, and have it in abundance (to the full, till it overflows)." I don't see any room for fear in that formula!

God wants us to stop depending on our own abilities alone and start confessing the truth of Philippians 4:13: "I can do everything through him [Christ] who gives me strength" (NIV). God wants us to have faith not only in His abilities but also in what He can and will accomplish *through* us.

Do It Afraid

Believing that and having faith will not always immediately take away the fear, but we shouldn't let that stop us. When we feel God urging us to try something new and different, we must step out and do it. Doing something new always requires a measure of faith. We must learn to confront our fears, and sometimes that means we must begin doing things while we are afraid.

Joyce Meyer relates an interesting story she read several years ago. She tells about a woman who was sharing with one of her Christian friends that all of her life she had been afraid. She was afraid to go out. She was afraid of people. She was afraid to drive. She told her friend that because she had been in such bondage to fear, she had never gone anywhere or done anything. She said, "I just have all these fears, and I don't know what to do." Her friend looked at her and said, "Well, do it afraid!"

Joyce wrote:
Reading that story was life-changing for me. I had a misconceived notion that I had to pray my fearful feelings away...and that I had to keep praying for God to deliver me

until those feelings were all gone. But that story helped me. And I have since learned that I don't have to bow down to those fearful feelings. I learned that I could do the things God wanted me to do...even while I was afraid. If I hadn't learned that lesson, I wouldn't be teaching and preaching today.

When you learn to trust God and step out even though you're afraid, God will provide the courage and boldness you need to overcome your fear. Just remember that there are no failures in Christ. If you make a mistake, God will just lift you up, teach you something from it, and send you on your way. You have not failed until you stop trying. So stop babysitting fear and make a decision to make some courageous and bold moves...even if you have to do it afraid!

God Is Perfect but We Are Not

As Christians, we know that it is God's plan for us to walk according to His good plan for our lives, without being encumbered with fear or doubt. However, so often I hear double-talk from some Christians, which indicates that they haven't really bought into who Christ is, who we as Christians are, and how Christ works in our lives.

Some say they believe that God is perfect, makes no mistakes, and is all-knowing, yet they turn right around and make statements or show by their actions that they don't believe that at all. For example, they say, "How can God call someone to a specific ministry and then later change His mind?" He doesn't!

Do you believe an all-knowing God works that way? Does He not know the purpose for each one of us? Does He make mistakes? The answer is a resounding NO! We, as human beings, are the ones who make mistakes. And the mistakes we make begin with our thinking.

There are two things that might have happened when it appears that God has changed His mind. Sometimes people might mistake their desire to do a certain thing for God as His calling. In their zeal to be His servants, they might choose to work in specific areas that are not a part of His perfect plan for them. In these cases, God not only will use these times as building blocks for these individuals, but He will gently prod them onto a path that leads them into His perfect plan. He uses His divine influence to direct them toward the position where they can be most effective. These people should never feel like a failure or be deterred from living God's perfect plan, because, as I mentioned earlier, He has a way of making everything "work together for the good of those who love God and are called according to his purpose for them" (Romans 8:28 NLT). If you really believe this, it will change the way you feel about some of the things you have done in the past.

The other thing that sometimes happens is God will use people for a time in certain positions to accomplish specific purposes. When those purposes are accomplished, He will move them into another area. If they are sensitive and obedient to God's leading, they will allow Him to use them wherever and however He desires. They will become confident that they can trust Him because they know He *never* makes a mistake. He cannot because He is truly God.

At some point in these scenarios, the individuals might

begin to doubt their spiritual discernment, and become fearful about "trying again." But when those fears and doubts flood in, they must remember that God can guide them toward His will for their lives.

If you have had such an experience in your own life, the truth presented here should restore your confidence in the God who never makes mistakes.

It is good to remember how God worked in the lives of men like Joseph, Jonah, Moses, Paul, and others. I'm sure you would agree that He did what *He* chose to do in their lives to accomplish His God-created purposes for them. "Free will" and "free choice" — which we hear so much about today — were not options for these men...nor can they be for those who are passionate about following God's call for their lives today.

Think about it — our loving Creator, the all-knowing, all-inspiring, ever-present, perfect God, cares so much about us that He offers His divine influence to help us make right decisions. Skeptics might argue that if that were the case, we would be perfect and make all the right decisions. But I don't agree.

God could have created us that way, had He chosen to do so, but I don't find any scriptural basis that leads me to believe that was His intention. The Bible tells me that as human beings we will fail and make bad decisions that will cause us to despair. But we also find that through those experiences, we will learn and grow.

God is more interested in us becoming more like Him than in our successes. Do you think a life full of successes would make you more like God? Or is it more likely that enduring some failures in life would make you more like Him? The answer is pretty obvious.

If God's plan had been for us to have lives without failure, He could have made that happen. But instead He gave us the freedom to choose, knowing that we would make some bad choices and experience failures. But He also knew that we would discover our need for Him because of those failures — and that through that process we would become more like Him.

Far better is it to dare mighty things, to win glorious triumphs, even though checkered by failure, than to take rank with those poor spirits who neither enjoy much nor suffer much, because they live in the gray twilight that knows neither victory nor defeat.

— **Theodore Roosevelt**

Get this straight in your thinking — we do have the "freedom to choose," but not "free will" or "free choice." There is a big difference. When we exercise our "freedom to choose," there are consequences for wrong choices. However, if we had "free will" and "free choice," there would be no consequences for any of our choices. When we accept salvation, we give up our will — what we want — in order to serve our Savior and live in His perfect will. And that's the only truly fulfilling choice. Did God make a mistake by creating us the way he did? No. God is perfect. He always has been and always will be. He calls us, as Christians, to become like Him, but it is a process that happens as we learn from our mistakes.

In his perennial Christian bestseller, *My Utmost for His Highest*, Oswald Chambers tells us, "Joy comes from seeing the complete fulfillment of the specific purpose for which I was created and born again, *not from successfully doing something of my own choosing.*"

God knew from the beginning that we would be imperfect individuals — He created us, and He is all knowing. He knew we would make mistakes — that's why He sent His Son, Jesus, to die for our sins. Through His sacrifice, we can be made righteous as we surrender our will to Him and are born again. Then we can have confidence that God is always with us. He is with us whether we believe it or not, so we may as well believe it and enjoy life!

As we submit to God and allow Him to have complete liberty in our lives, He will lead, guide, and direct our steps.

If you have allowed your dreams to be buried by your fear of failure, it is time to make a change. Two thousand years ago, the philosopher Seneca said, "If we let things terrify us, life is not worth living." And that is still true today. So don't let fear rob you of being a success in life. As you submit to God and allow Him to have complete liberty in your life, He will lead, guide, and direct your steps.

In his book, *Wild at Heart*, John Eldredge quotes fellow author Howard Macey: "The spiritual life cannot be made suburban. It is always frontier and we who live in it must accept and even rejoice that it remains untamed."

That word "untamed" is a powerful adjective, especially when used to describe our potential. It is not the future that is untamed; it is really the present. Are we willing to see our present failures as the future successes they are meant to be?

John Eldredge says, "The greatest obstacle to realizing our dreams is the false self's hatred of mystery."

The good news is that failure is not a mystery; it is predictable, dependable, and consistent. But the most important thing for us to remember is that it is not the end; instead, it is *only the beginning*— the beginning of an exciting opportunity for us to grow.

QUESTIONS FOR REFLECTION & DISCUSSION

1. In what way did the writer John Milton feel that he failed?
2. To what ambition did Socrates hold?
3. Why do most people fear failure?
4. What is the result of failure?
7. Why does the author say fear is something to enthusiastically embrace?
6. We really only fail when?
7. The author relates the story of Cyrus W. Field and his numerous attempts (and failures) to lay a transatlantic cable. What drove Mr. Field to continue trying after so many failed attempts?
8. How can you apply Mr. Field's philosophy to your own life?
9. Winston Churchill is quoted as saying, "Success is going from failure to failure without losing enthusiasm."
    *   How does that statement relate to what the Apostle Paul wrote in Philippians 3:14: "I press toward the mark for the prize of the high calling of God in Christ Jesus"
10. The author quotes Howard Macey: "The spiritual life cannot be made suburban. It is always frontier and we who live in it must accept and even rejoice that it remains untamed."
11. What does Macey mean by that statement?
12. What is the most important thing for us to remember about failure?

POINTS FOR REVIEW

*   Failure is not the end; only an exciting opportunity for us to grow.
*   Failure is something to enthusiastically embrace.
*   When we choose to rid ourselves of our fear of failing, we find that we are willing to risk more, do more, give more of ourselves, and be more.

*The problem is never how to get new,
innovative thoughts into your mind,
but how to get old ones out.*

— Dee Hock

CHAPTER FOUR

Envision Limits

Of all the properties which
belong to honorable men,
not one is so highly prized
as that of character.

— Henry Clay

L ife is full of opportunities, but none are more important than those times when we find our-selves at a crossroads — faced with making a choice that will send a strong message to others about who we are and how we see our life and its purpose. I faced such a crossroads in 1964.

While working as an insurance adjustor in Ardmore, Oklahoma, I was assigned my own territory, which was unusual for someone as young as I was then. When I took the job, I was given strict instructions that there was one agent in particular that I had to "keep happy." His name was Mr. Hensley. He had a large agency, which meant he had the power and ability to refer us a lot of business, should he choose to do so.

One day, I received an emergency call from Mr. Hensley, saying I was needed in Sapulpa immediately. This was an unusual request, but since it was Mr. Hensley, I dropped what I was doing and went right then — remembering during the drive that I "needed to keep Mr. Hensley happy."

When I arrived at the local Chevrolet dealership, it immediately became obvious to me that there was a serious water leak coming from the roof of the building — a building owned by the vice president of a local bank. After inspecting the building and determining the problem, I explained to Mr. Hensley that the contractor had done his "inspection" and concluded that the leak was caused by a "settling" problem, which meant the damage was not covered by the insurance policy. Mr. Hensley turned to the banker and asked if he would be satisfied with the insurance company paying only 50 percent of what it would cost to make the necessary repairs. Of course, the banker said yes, having just learned that his insurance policy really didn't cover the damages.

I was then directed by Mr. Hensley to pay 50 percent of the claim. I responded by saying that if I was going to pay any of the claim, I would just as soon pay all of it, but since it wasn't covered by the policy, I would not be able to pay any of it. Mr. Hensley grew red with anger.

Consider at this point the possibility that fear could have had something to do with Mr. Hensley's anger. Could he have been fearful about losing a good customer…or of losing his reputation of being able to get his client's claims paid even when they were not covered? Then consider whether or not Mr. Hensley would have responded in anger to my response had he been living by faith and trusting God with his life.

My Crossroads Decision

Mr. Hensley then suggested that it would be a good idea for us to go to lunch together. After taking a couple of steps, I stopped and told him that I had something I needed to do over lunch, which was very true. I had to get alone with myself, to do some serious thinking. I had to decide the answers to some difficult questions. Was I really going to risk losing my job? Was I going to stand by my belief that God was in charge of my life and trust that He would tell me what to do? After some intense contemplation, I made my decision. If it were necessary, I would risk losing my job. I chose faith over the fear which most likely would have caused me to make the opposite decision.

After lunch, I met Mr. Hensley and the banker at the bank as instructed. Once again, I explained that according to the insurance policy, the damages were not covered, and that I could not submit the claim. I went on to say that requesting payment would have required me to lie to the insurance company about the cause of the damage, and I wasn't willing to do that.

Mr. Hensley, more than a little upset about my decision, said, "So you're not any smarter now than you were before lunch?"

With my stomach in knots, I swallowed hard and replied, "I guess not." Then I addressed the banker, "I have explained to you that, based on your policy, you are not entitled to any payment. Knowing that, how much do you want me to pay you?"

After a few moments of contemplation, he quietly responded, "Nothing."

At the time, I really had not considered how that outcome might make the agent look, but it didn't take long for me to discover his reaction. On my next visit to his office — after refusing to pay the loss claim on the banker's building — he avoided me, telling me through his secretary that he had no referrals for me. This continued for three weeks in a row.

On the fourth week, I asked Mr. Hensley's secretary if I might visit with Mr. Hensley. The door to his office was open, and I could see that he was in. As his secretary buzzed him on the phone, I moved to his office door, and said, "Mr. Hensley, I know why you are unhappy with me and why you are not giving me any business...and I even understand." Asking for just a moment of his time, I quickly made my point. "Several weeks ago, you mentioned to me that you had a son about my age, and you told me how proud you were of your son. And I'm wondering, Mr. Hensley, if someone put your son in the same position that you put me in — one that would require him to compromise his values and integrity — what would you want your son to do?"

It was obvious that my question had hit the mark, capturing Mr. Hensley's attention and giving him a new perspective of the situation. His eyes grew moist, he swallowed hard, and with great courage and humility, he asked me to forgive him.

We taught one another great lessons that day. I reminded him that a man's integrity must have value, or he will begin to sell pieces of himself until there is nothing left. He taught me that when you make a mistake, it takes enormous courage to recognize it and ask for forgiveness.

I got all of Mr. Hensley's business after that day. Is that beautiful or what?

The important thing to learn from this example is that fear could have caused me to compromise my values and destroy my Christian witness, but thank God, I knew what I had to do.

Did I meet God's terms by taking a stand for my Christian beliefs? Did God honor that? The obvious answer is yes. But what if I had allowed fear to take over? This was my first job out of college, and I had a wife and baby to support. And I had no savings. From a natural standpoint things didn't look too good, but I knew that I had a wealthy Father who had promised to meet all my needs, so I chose to trust Him. If you are a Christian, you have a wealthy Father who wants to meet all your needs too — so trust Him!

> *Our doubts are traitors, and make us lose the good we oft might win by fearing to attempt.*
> **— William Shakespeare**

Bill McCartney, founder of Promise Keepers, once said in a message to a crowd of 2,000 men and boys: "Your best days are ahead if you meet God's terms." He went on to explain that God has terms, and that we can only come into His kingdom "on God's terms."

I have learned that God's terms require us to always trust Him and live in faith instead of fear — *always!* We can only live the abundant life of peace, joy, and excitement, when we live according to "His terms."

Most people will tell you to envision a limitless future, but I would remind you of the importance of knowing your limits. It is just as important to envision your limits as your dreams…and doing so does not limit your potential, dreams, purpose, and talents. Rather, it enables you to choose to draw the lines of demarcation in your life. I have heard it said that if you stand for nothing, you will fall for almost anything, and I don't think any of us want that for our lives.

Setting Limits

Setting limits for ourselves is our God-given right and responsibility. It shapes and defines our moral values and determines how we live our lives. Eleanor Roosevelt made a wise statement about this topic: "Remember always that you not only have the right to be an individual, you have an obligation to be one."

As we set the parameters that define our character, we must include God in the process, listening for that still small voice that will guide us in the process. Some obvious considerations are setting limits on the value we place on our time and health. We must acknowledge and honor our value as a human being and recognize our intrinsic self-worth. Setting such limits reduces stress and makes life more enjoyable — conditions that not only benefit us but also those around us.

Setting limits also frees us from any tendencies to be "people pleasers," a common problem in our society today. Some people compromise their own desires and plans in order to gain the approval of others because they fear being rejected. "People pleasing" is a terrible tyranny, and it certainly is not God's plan for our lives. We must make choices based on what *we* believe, not what others believe — setting whatever limits are necessary for us to be at peace with who we are inside.

We must do what is right even though it may not always be popular or easy. Standing for what is right is a true test of moral character. That is what God requires of us...and we should expect it of ourselves. When we violate ourselves by not doing what we know to be right, we betray ourselves and create havoc in our lives.

I had the opportunity to share this information with my driver one day as he was taking me to the airport. He had cut through a business parking lot in order to make a left-hand turn. I asked him, "If you were stopped by a police officer, could you honestly say you were doing the right thing?" He got a little defensive, but when he calmed down, I brought it up again in a non-threatening way, and he admitted that he would have to say no.

I then shared with him that he had betrayed himself, compromising his integrity and creating a potential for havoc in his life. I assured him that we all betray ourselves sometimes, and pointed out the need of being honest with ourselves and with God in these situations. It will make our lives more enjoyable if we can just get rid of fear and admit it when we are wrong. If we are honest with God and ask Him to forgive us, He will. And He will help us establish limits for ourselves that help us avoid making the same mistakes again.

In talking about setting limits, there is an important thing we must remember — we must be careful that we don't settle for smaller visions. We may be tempted to keep life pared down to our human limitations, but we must be careful to focus on God and His strategy for us. He calls us to greatness, and that involves strong convictions that cannot be compromised and actions that are a result of our faith. There are no limits to what we can accomplish with God's help, and we must remain open to His leading.

We must not surrender our self-worth to the opinions and judgments of others…nor should we hedge our convictions and adjust our values to suit them. When we get it right — when we find just the right parameters for our lives — we gain a liberating perspective that brings us peace.

Maintaining Integrity

If you are an Internet user, then you are likely familiar with the popular search engine, Google. If you were to type in the name, Reuben Gonzalez, you would find the story that I am about to share. I tell it exactly as I found it, because though the author is unknown, it's a terrific story that beautifully illustrates my point about the importance of individual integrity.

> If you go as far as you can see, you will then see enough to go even farther.
> — John Wooden

"A while back, there was a story about Reuben Gonzalez, who was in the final match of his first professional racquetball tournament. He was playing the perennial champion for his first shot at a victory on the pro circuit. At match point in the fifth and final game, Gonzalez made a super "kill shot" into the front corner to win the tournament. The referee called it good, and one of the linemen confirmed that the shot was a winner.

"But after a moment's hesitation, Gonzalez turned
and declared that his shot had skipped into the wall,
hitting the floor first. As a result, the serve went to his
opponent, who went on to win the match.

"Reuben Gonzalez walked off the court; everyone was stunned. The next issue of a leading racquetball magazine featured Gonzalez on its cover.
The lead editorial searched and questioned for an
explanation for the occurrence on the professional
racquetball circuit. Who could ever imagine it in any
sport or endeavor? Here was a player with everything
officially in his favor, with victory in his grasp, who
disqualified himself at match point and lost.

"When asked why he did it, Gonzalez replied,
'It was the only thing I could do to maintain my
integrity.'"

Yes, maintaining our integrity is of utmost importance,
for without it nothing else really matters.

After studying top achievers and peak performers for
many years, I have concluded that their success stems, in
great part, from their ability to discern what they should
limit and eliminate and what they should keep and strength-
en. One obvious thing that should be eliminated is fear,
because it limits one's options.

Calm Amid the Chaos

Sometimes in life we are dealt such horrifying situations
that fear would seem to be the only appropriate response. For
instance, in times of war, disaster, death, or traumatic injury,
fear is often considered to be natural — the only option. My
friend, Todd Huston, suffered such an experience.

While enjoying some fun in the sun, fourteen-year-old Todd was untangling the ski rope behind the family boat when the motor slipped into reverse. His screams for the driver to stop the boat, which was heading directly toward him, could not be heard over the sounds of the motor and the churning water. As he frantically tried to swim away from the path of the boat, the propellers grabbed him, mangling his legs as he struggled to stay above water.

When his father pulled him into the boat, they were met with the horrifying sight of muscle and bone hanging from Todd's legs. As Todd watched the blood spurting from one of his femoral arteries, he had to quickly remind himself that he had a choice about how he would react. He could do what would seem to be the most obvious, given the situation, and give in to the fear that was trying desperately to grip his mind and emotions — or he could choose to do what he had been told numerous times as a Boy Scout, "Do not panic." Todd chose the latter.

In addition to his physical pain and trauma, there was blood everywhere, and other people on the boat were getting sick — but Todd remained calm despite the chaos. The wise action of this fourteen-year-old boy and the grace of God are probably what saved his life. Think about how different the outcome might have been if Todd had given in to fear.

After spending months in the hospital, and going through many painful surgeries, Todd finally left the hospital. He had severe damage to both legs, and suffered a permanently paralyzed right leg. He didn't realize how close he had come to losing his life until years later, when he read the hospital report that noted he had to be resuscitated twice during surgery due to massive blood loss.

For many less-determined young men, this injury could have spelled the end of a vibrant life and any hope of an athletic career. But not for Todd Huston. This was only the beginning of his story. The paralyzed leg was a continuous problem and, like a diabetic with an ulcerated foot, Todd faced possible amputation. When the doctors told Todd that he had two choices: years of skin graph surgeries — which would stop him from pursuing his education and living a normal life — or amputation. He chose to have a life instead of a leg.

Assurance from God

Todd recalls how he feared the surgery that would change his life forever. "I can remember looking out my hospital window at the moon shining on the river below. It was then that God assured me that He would be by my side throughout this devastating experience."

Todd bravely went to surgery, and the physicians amputated his leg. Todd says he now knows from personal experience that fear is a choice, and that choosing God over fear is always the best choice. "I had to know that the power within me was much greater than the power in the world," Todd says. "God is greater than any of our fears." Todd chose to trust in God instead of believing his fears.

Todd pursued his education, earned a degree in psychology, and became a psychotherapist. But it is his personal experience that has enabled him to provide understanding and effective counseling for patients and families who have faced devastating disabilities. Through his writing, seminars, and speeches, Todd has brought hope to many. But Todd is not just a man of words — he is a man who believes in action.

Todd was asked to join a team of other disabled people who aspired to climb to the highest point of each of the fifty states. He trained for a year, until the project fell through because of a lack of sponsorship. Instead of quitting and making excuses as to why he was not going on the expedition, he sought out his own sponsorship, continued training for the climb, and organized the expedition. This was in spite of never having done anything like this before. Todd didn't allow fear to back him down — he faced it head-on.

Todd said, "I had moments of fear about what I was getting myself into. After all, only thirty-two people in the world had accomplished this, and a leg amputee had never done anything like this before. I would be the first." He overcame his temporary fear by facing it and applying his faith. "I had to keep believing that this was God's plan."

Todd to the Top!

With little if any real mountain-climbing experience, Todd took off in a pickup truck loaded with camping gear, and began a 24,000-mile trip throughout the United States. He navigated to the highest points of each state. Some high points were literally a bump in the road, like the high point of Delaware, or a spot on the prairie in Kansas. However, others were much more dangerous — places where Todd witnessed rescuers dragging the dead bodies of able-bodied climbers in front of him. He summitted the highest mountains in North America, including the volcanoes of Mt. Rainier and Mt. Hood, the Rocky Mountains, Sierra Nevadas, and Appalachians. He scaled 1,000-foot cliffs, hiked up 14,000-foot mountains, and traversed through snow and rock avalanches — enough to acquaint any man with fear. But each and every time, he chose faith.

Perhaps Todd's greatest climb was Mt. McKinley. At 20,320 feet, it is the highest mountain in North America. The mountain has crevasses below, and avalanches from above. The air is thin enough to make your brain swell and cause you to die, if the sub-zero temperatures don't freeze you first.

Todd recalls having panic attacks before flying into base camp. "This is one time when I tried to hide my fear instead of dealing with it. This caused my mind and body to react in unhealthy ways. I was truly petrified with fear. I was so scared that I could barely keep moving." Todd knew that he could turn around and quit, but instead, he chose to face his fear and overcome it. He now realizes that you don't "deal" with fear by denying it or avoiding it. You either choose it or you don't. If you choose fear, then you become its slave. He states, "I have since realized that fear is a choice, and you must choose the only other option, which is God."

Todd Huston did finish climbing the highest points of all fifty states. He not only became the first leg amputee to climb all fifty high points, but he also shattered the world record by 35 days, a record that has yet to be broken. This man — whose heart had stopped beating twice, and whose leg had been removed, giving him little hope of ever walking again — is the only disabled person to hold an able-bodied world record in mountaineering, one of the most extreme sports. Todd was able to accomplish all of this because he faced his fear each step of the way…until he reached the top.

I will forever be grateful to my friend Todd for allowing me to share his inspiring story in this book. I'm sure you were blessed as you visualized him facing fear and choosing faith that enabled him to master the challenge of each and every mountain. I pray that you will follow Todd's example by choosing faith instead of fear when you face the mountains in your own life.

Peak performers in all areas of life choose to limit their fear, impulsivity, anger, and their habit to procrastinate. They limit their negative self-talk, their entitled self-consumed perspectives, their complaints, and their excuses. When you envision yourself putting limits on the things that limit you, you become free to live the limitless potential that God has for your life.

Many ask, "What are the things that will open up my life to unlimited possibilities, and what do I have to limit in order to achieve my goals?"

Perhaps you can find the answers in the concepts I jokingly call: What You "C" Is What You Get. In these seven C's of success, you will discover what you need to limit and eliminate, as well as what you need to keep and create more of in your life. You will easily C how these recommendations can, and will, feed your success.

What You C Is What You Get

1. You must *limit your confusion* in order to create *Clarity*. More than 80 percent of your success stems from being clear about who you are, what you believe in, what you stand for, and what you want. This requires that you ask yourself two of the most important questions any human being asks of themselves: "Who am I?" and "What is the purpose for my life?" When you have carefully

answered these very vital questions, your direction becomes clear, your path opens before you, and the work of your soul begins.

2. You must *limit words with no value.* Only say what you mean, and mean what you say. This strengthens your integrity and fills your life with *Congruency.* Most obstacles to success come from within. Once you gain clarity about *who* you are, and what you believe and want, it is important to build the character and integrity that are necessary to act congruently with whom you see and *speak* yourself to be. This includes making a commitment to becoming aware of any negative thoughts or talk that you cling to in your life. When you are clear, you can be congruent with your thoughts, your words, and your actions.

3. You must *limit your areas of weakness* and develop more *Competence.* You can't climb to the next rung on the ladder until you develop a true competence where you are presently. Competence is tied to continual learning and encompasses a willingness to become an expert at whatever you desire. Competence asks that we learn about those who have excelled before us — that we study and emulate the greatness we are dedicated to and striving for.

4. You must *limit unnecessary or distracting options* and strengthen your *Concentration.* As previously discussed, too many options actually distract you. The ability to focus on one thing,

single-mindedly, and see it through until it is done, takes character and discipline. Developing your ability to focus literally multiplies your chances for success.

5. You must **limit excuses** and unchain your **Creativity**. Whenever you feel stuck, you need to flood your life with ideas from many sources. Creativity needs to be exercised like a muscle — if you don't use it, you will lose it. Challenge yourself to "think outside the box." Attempt to look at things from many different perspectives, and be open to new ideas. Don't waste time making excuses for present failures. Instead, use your experiences, both bad and good, in new, innovative, and creative ways that will help mold you into the person you dream of becoming. Never, never, never think of yourself as a victim to anyone except God. Seeing yourself as a victim is the most destructive barrier to personal growth.

6. You must **limit your fear** and live your life with **Courage**. This is the main theme of this book. You must choose to be courageous as you live your life. Living a life of great faith requires courage. Courage is in great demand. It is the willingness to do the things that you know are right simply because they are right, no matter what the consequences may be. Courage is not about feelings — it is about action. It is about feeling the fear and choosing the path of faith that will enable you to do what you need to do in spite of how fear would love to stop you.

7. You must *limit the time you spend watching television* and dedicate yourself instead to *Continuous Learning.* In addition to your regular time spent in reading God's Word, read at least one good book a week. Schedule some time to learn how to use the World Wide Web. When used wisely, the Internet is a wonderful resource that can open a whole new world of learning to you. Along with reading and researching on the Web, listen to great books on audiotape as you drive in your car. Read books aloud with your children or grandchildren. The time you invest in reading will pay huge dividends. *Not all readers are leaders, but all leaders are readers.*

Successful people discern what needs to be limited and what needs to be strengthened in order for their companies, organizations, churches, and families to succeed. Success isn't magic. It isn't a secret reserved for an elite few. It simply requires a willingness and firm resolve that you will allow nothing to stand in the way of realizing your dream.

I encourage you to stand for something strong and true, something that will live on in the hearts of your children. There are values, philosophies, doctrines, and standards that define greatness, but if you are to stay committed to the ideals you cherish, there will be times when you must envision and stand up for the limits you set for yourself.

Success is neither magical or mysterious. Success is the natural consequence of consistently applying the basic fundamentals.

— Jim Rohn

QUESTIONS FOR REFLECTION & DISCUSSION

1. The author states in chapter four: "A man's life must have value or he will begin to sell pieces of himself until there is nothing left." What does that statement mean to you?

2. Instead of envisioning a limitless future, the author reminds us to know our limits; that they are as important to envision as our dreams. Why?

3. The success of top achievers and peak performers is the result of what two things?

4. When you envision yourself placing limits around the things that limit you, what can happen?

5. In studying the seven C's of success, the first one is Clarity. Why is it important to be clear about who you are?

6. The mathematical definition of *congruent* is "having the same size and shape." How does this definition correspond to what you think and say, and the sort of person you seek to be?

7. From where do most obstacles to success come?

8. What one thing can you do to strengthen your integrity?

9. Once you know who you are and what you are about, what is the next important step?

10. How do negative thoughts and talk get in the way of becoming the person you want to be?

11. The author states that you must "limit your areas of weakness and develop more competence."
    *   In what area of your life should you begin to develop more competence?
    *   How will strengthening this particular area of your life help you in other areas?
    *   What sort of fear did not allow you to work on this area before now?

12. Concentration is the fourth C to success. Developing the ability to focus on one thing single-mindedly, and see it

through until it's done takes what two things?

- How are these two traits related?
- Is it possible to have one without the other?
- Why or why not?

13. Webster defines *creativity* as being "inventive or imaginative." This definition suggests that it is necessary for us to "think outside the box," as the author states, without wasting time "making excuses for present failures." He encourages us to use our experiences, both good and bad, in new, innovative and creative ways to help us become the person we dream of becoming.

- What life experiences, good or bad, can you use in a creative way to help you become the person you dream of becoming?

14. The sixth C is Courage. To quote Shakespeare: "Our doubts are traitors, and make us lose the good we oft might win by fearing to attempt." Courage is not about feelings; it is about action. Name one area of your life in which you "fear to attempt" and need to take action.

15. The last C is Continuous Learning. The author suggests limiting our time watching television and instead committing to reading at least one book a week. Learning to use the Internet as a learning tool and listening to great books as we drive are also encouraged. To quote him: "Not all readers are leaders, but all leaders are readers."

- Why is reading and continuing to learn so important?

16. According to the author, on what is success dependent?

Points for Review

- ▶ A man's life must have value or he will begin to sell pieces of himself until there is nothing left.
- ▶ Envision your limits.
- ▶ Success is the natural consequence of consistently applying the basic fundamentals.

Example is leadership.

— Dr. Albert Schweitzer

CHAPTER FIVE

Attitude Is Never Enough

It is time for us all to stand and cheer for the
doer, the achiever — the one who recognizes
the challenge and does something about it.

— Vince Lombardi

O ne of the premier NCAA college coaches of his era, Lou Holtz said, "Ability is what you're capable of doing. Motivation determines what you do. Attitude determines how well you do it." But the game of football can't be played until the players suit up and line up on the field. Yes, our attitudes are important, even contagious, but why? They are contagious because we act them out in the world. We *act* them out with every snap of the ball of life.

We have heard it said, time and time again, that "attitude is everything." I disagree. I say that "attitude is *not enough.*" It is true that our attitudes dramatically affect our thought processes, which in turn dramatically affect the actions we choose to take, but our attitudes alone are not enough. Our *actions* actually have the most powerful and dramatic effect on those with whom we come in contact. If we share acts of kindness, respect, honor, and compassion, everyone involved is positively impacted by those acts, including us. These positive acts can cause a chain-reaction effect that is astounding. With each casual contact, phone conversation, and e-mail message, it spreads. The people who are infected by our actions infect others, who then pass it on to still others. As these powerful actions quickly spread each day throughout our world, they make a positive difference everywhere they happen.

A psychologist I visited with a few years ago, gave me information that confirms this. He said people can take on another person's anger if they are around them long enough. I had some difficulty accepting that until he told me that it works the same way with love.

That's an awesome thought. Just think of the potential we have for spreading love, faith, and all kinds of good things! What about you? What will you spread around to others? Will it be anger, the product of fear...or love, the product of faith?

Acting in Faith

You probably heard the news story about a twenty-six-year-old single mom in Atlanta who was forced into her house and tied up at gunpoint by a murder suspect. That's probably one of the most frightening things that could happen to a person, but this woman — who had just read a book about God's purpose in our lives — was able to act out of her faith in God rather than out of her very justifiable fear.

She calmly talked her captor into untying her so she could fix him breakfast and read to him from the Bible and from a book she had read entitled *The Purpose Driven Life*, written by Pastor Rick Warren. She convinced the man that God had a purpose for his life, even in his present situation, and eventually convinced him to give himself up to the authorities.

This woman's knowledge of God's Word allowed her to overcome fear by appropriating faith and showing God's love to another human being who, according to the world's standards, did not deserve it. However, God's love does not discriminate. For our redemption, He sent His son to suffer a cruel death on a cross — and none of us deserved it. We are all recipients of God's undeserved love, and as His representatives on earth, it is our responsibility to share that love.

This single mom could have freaked out, with disastrous results. But instead of giving in to fear, she chose to believe that there was a purpose for the encounter. She gained courage as she began to act, trusting God with the outcome.

> It's easier to act your way into a new way of thinking than to think your way into a new way of acting.
>
> — Millard Fuller
> Founder of Habitat for Humanity

I think we can all be encouraged by this story, knowing that God will provide that same kind of courage to get us through whatever frightening situation we may be facing if only we will choose faith instead of fear. We just have to activate our faith instead of allowing fear to control us.

There are times in life when we face what we consider to be a challenge without recognizing it as an opportunity to display attitudes and actions that are a testimony of our Christian faith. I once faced just such a challenge and opportunity with one of my neighbors.

Mr. Robertson had always been "unfriendly," but I came home from work one day to learn that he had displayed his "unfriendliness" in a rather unusual way. He had called a light company to move a light pole from his yard to mine. The pole had been in his yard for years, long before I moved next door, but he said it was supposed to be on my property.

I was interested in knowing what the problem was. So one day when I saw him in his back yard, I took advantage of the opportunity. I went over and in a friendly and non-threatening manner, I asked Mr. Robertson — a man twenty years my senior — what was bothering him. I wanted to try to understand why he was acting the way he was and see if there was anything I could do to help us become "friendly" neighbors. He didn't know what to think of my question, but he decided to take the opportunity to "set me straight" about a few things.

He first expressed anger about our kids' dog, making it clear that he wanted us to get rid of it because he didn't like it coming into his yard. He also wanted us to get rid of the kids' chickens, which we kept cooped up. He said that even though we lived in the country, he didn't think chickens belonged in our yard. And finally, he let me know that he had a complaint about the gravel driveway leading to our house. He informed me that it extended across his property, and (even though it had been there before we moved in) he now wanted to put up a fence, so I would need to move the drive.

At first I stood there stunned. How could this man think I would take him seriously? He was being incredibly selfish and stubborn. But after taking a moment to consider his point of view, I told him that we would make the changes he had requested. I said we would get rid of the dog and the chickens right way, but that I would need a few days to take care of the driveway, which Mr. Robertson understood.

When I discussed the situation with my wife and children, they were understandably upset. But I explained to them that if we truly believed and lived our faith, it called for us to show the love of God to our neighbor. If our lives were to be good examples, it would require more from us than just lip service. It was really tough for the children, but they came to understand and agree that these were the right things to do. Even though it was a sad evening at the Richardson home, we all knew that we had made the right decision.

> The smallest actual good is better than the most magnificent promise of impossibilities.
> — Thomas Babington Macaulay

Early the next morning, when there was a knock on the door, we couldn't imagine who would be coming by at thta time of day. When I answered the door, Mr. Robertson was standing there. His words were a real surprise: "I have come to tell you that when I made those requests yesterday, I was speaking out of frustration and anger, and I would like for you to disregard them. I want you to keep your dog and chickens, and your driveway is fine where it is."

Wow! That made me wonder where fear would have taken us, and what kind of example it would have been for our children…as well as Mr. Robertson.

We lived there for many years, side by side, and had a great relationship that actually turned into a friendship. This is just a case in point, to show that attitude is not enough. We had to be willing not only to tell our neighbor we loved him, but to also display that love, even in tough and potentially costly situations.

On another occasion, I had the opportunity to help a man who had settled for far less than his dream. Because he hadn't chosen faith over fear and developed the proper attitude about successfully achieving his dream, Shorty was unable to take positive action. God gave me a plan, and I acted on it.

When, at the age of twenty-six, I became sales manager for a national insurance company in Houston, Texas, the first agent I hired was a man named Shorty Thompson. Shorty was a likable man, a good man, and as I spent time with him, training him to sell insurance, we became good friends.

Don't Settle for Second Best

As I spent time with Shorty, I learned that his lifelong dream was to become a schoolteacher and coach. But Shorty, I soon learned, had always looked for a "convenient" time to follow his dream. He had decided to just settle for whatever life brought to him, rather than taking a risk and going for his dream. Even though selling wasn't the best choice for Shorty, he did his job, but he did it mostly out of sheer determination. He didn't really enjoy it.

One night I had trouble sleeping. As I lay there in bed, thinking about Shorty, I knew that he was white-knuckling his way through this sales job. And even though he was selling and reaching his goals, I knew that he was miserable. After contemplating the situation much of the night in an effort to find the right solution, I finally decided on a plan.

I got out of bed at 1:00 A.M. and drove to Shorty's house. I knocked on his door and invited him to go with me to get a cup of coffee. Shorty was a bit confused about what was going on, but he agreed to go with me. After our coffee had been served, I attempted to explain to Shorty that even though I had what I considered to be good reasons for doing what I was about to do, it was most probably going to anger him. All I could hope for was that one day he would understand and, hopefully, thank me for it.

I gave Shorty a thirty-day notice of termination. I explained to him that I believed in him and his lifelong dream, and I pointed out that he wasn't doing me, the company, or himself any favors by settling for a job that could never fulfill his career dream. I encouraged Shorty to see this situation as a great opportunity for him to finally do what he had dreamed of doing for many years. It was the most difficult decision I had ever had to make up to that point in my short career as a manager, but I knew that I had Shorty's best interest in mind. That's the thing that gave me the strength I needed to follow through with my plan.

Of course, Shorty didn't understand my thinking, and he certainly wasn't happy with me. In fact, he was angrier than I had ever imagined he would be. Shorty would even cross the street to avoid speaking to me. But he did take advantage of the opportunity I had given him by taking action. He went back to college, got his degree, and became a teacher and a coach. He has thanked me many times for what I did that night.

Shorty discovered what I already knew — that attitude is never enough. He learned from experience that he had to be willing to overcome his fears and take actions that would move him toward his dreams. When he overcame his fear and took action, Shorty finally realized his dreams.

Plan for Success

As a young boy, I knew that I wanted to invest my efforts in a career that would somehow help people and make a difference in their lives. For some reason, I always felt moved to help those who had been abused or taken advantage of in other ways. At that time, I had no concept of the major differences a trial lawyer could make in the lives of those who had been "stepped on" by the power structure. But here I am, years later — a trial lawyer. Beginning with that vague boyhood desire, I developed a clear career mission, and then I took steps to make it happen. Most of my professional goals have been directed toward the fulfillment of that mission.

When I began to see how people were being destroyed by fear, I began writing this book in my mind. The more I saw of fear, the more I realized that what I had learned from my dad years ago on our back porch was true — fear is never our friend. I know today that this book had been developing inside me since that time.

Over the years, I have continued to learn that maintaining a positive attitude allows me to concentrate on my missions and strategies for attaining my goals. I have learned that occupying my mind with thoughts of everything that could go wrong causes me to lose my focus.

Many people today live every day in a negative fog. They want something better, but because of fear and the distortion it brings, they have no clear plan of action to achieve it. They expect the worst and they are not surprised when it happens. I prefer to expect the best. A positive attitude is not just a "head in the clouds" cover-up that denies the existence of obstacles. It can, and most often does, indicate the existence of a strategy for success.

For example, when you are on a trip you may encounter unexpected obstacles along the way — bad weather, a bridge washed out, or a detour — but you can't let that stop you if you are determined to reach your destination. The same is true in every area of your life. You must move on to plan B, take whatever action is necessary to overcome the obstacles, and move along toward your destination.

If we are to see success in our lives, we must have a purpose and a plan and be willing to do whatever it takes to accomplish that purpose — even if it means overcoming obstacles. Sometimes obstacles can be frightening, and, sadly, many people succumb to that fear. Instead of finding a way to conquer the obstacle, they listen to the negative thoughts that warn them of impending failure. This kind of thinking can be, and most often is, fear — and most of the time, the things we fear never happen. Too often, when we allow fear to occupy our minds, it causes us to lose our ability to focus and move toward the accomplishment of our real mission.

I tell you again: Fear is *never* our friend!

Attitude, the Motivating Factor

Years ago, I heard a story about a company that made shoes. They sent a salesman to an underdeveloped country where they knew the people did not customarily wear shoes. The salesman, upon arriving in the country, immediately called his employer and complained, "There's been a big mistake. People in this country don't even wear shoes."

The company immediately brought the salesman back home. Then they sent another salesman who, upon arrival in the country, immediately called his employer with a great deal of excitement. "This is great!" he said. "Ship me more shoes. No one here has shoes."

What makes a good or bad territory for a salesman depends more on his attitude than on existing conditions.

This is an important lesson for all of us about attitudes and feelings. Our attitude plays a key role in whether we are motivated enough to take the necessary steps to become a success, and our attitude is greatly affected by whether we choose fear or faith.

> My dreams are worthless, my plans are dust, my goals are impossible. All are of no value unless they are followed by action. I will act now.
>
> — Og Mandino
> The Greatest Salesman in the World

We must not allow fear to keep us from taking action when we feel strongly about our purpose in life. When we find ourselves saying, "I would do such and such, but I'm afraid that…" it is time to stop and listen to what we are saying. Remember, fear is never your friend, so don't allow it to control any part of your life.

Will You Do Nothing...or Something?

Many people actually want to do something new and different to better their lives and the lives of others — but because they allow fear to dwell in their minds, they usually settle for doing nothing.

There are many fears that attack our minds and emotions, and if we give in to them they will render us weak and powerless. Millions of people never reach their full potential because of their fear of failure. Because of this debilitating fear, they choose to do nothing, opting to play it safe. As a result, the only thing they ever succeed at is nothing!

But it doesn't have to be that way. As we all know, faith is the opposite of fear, and when we activate our faith we can overcome fear's paralyzing effects. I believe it is much better to step out in faith and find out what you can do than to spend your life doing nothing and wondering what else you might have been able to accomplish. Don't be a part of the group that, in their old age, looks back on their life and wishes they had taken more risks.

We all are born with a destiny, and we can never successfully fulfill that destiny if we are afraid of trying something different. Is it risky? Yes. But we must be willing to take a chance on a negative experience if we are ever to reap the rewards of having a good one. Everything good in life depends on faith, so we must learn to step out in faith...even if we feel afraid.

Remember, I have never said we won't experience fear. What I do say — and you really need to get this — is that fear is never our friend. "Why is it so important to know that?" you might ask. It is important because once you truly know and accept that fear is never your friend, you will begin to take control over it in your life. As long as you believe that fear may benefit your life in some way, you will allow it to reside in you — but you'll never be able to make the distinction between beneficial and non-beneficial fear. Believe me — all fear is non-beneficial...with the exception of the fear of God, which we will discuss in chapter seven.

Do you remember the Bible story of David and Goliath? David was only a small boy, and the odds of him being able to kill the giant Goliath didn't look too good. But David refused to look at it that way. As Detroit author Bishop Andrew Merritt so aptly put it: "King Saul and his army said, 'The giant is so big — we can't defeat him.' But David, the shepherd boy, went out to face Goliath with a slingshot and a pocketful of rocks. And he said, 'The giant is so big — I can't possibly miss him.'"

David stepped out in faith, believing that the same God who had helped him overcome other dangerous situations would do it again. So he took action...and his faith combined with his action paid off! When he wound up that slingshot and the stone sailed through the air and hit its mark, Goliath was a defeated foe! (See Samuel 17.)

There is an important lesson here about where we should place our focus. David didn't focus on the massive size of Goliath and see it as a threat. He focused on the divine power of God — power that had enabled him to conquer seemingly hopeless situations in the past. When we quit focusing on our own inabilities and start focusing on the great things that God wants to do *through* us, it helps develop faith and a courageous spirit that empowers us to step out and do something meaningful. Fear will *always* cause you to focus on that which will rob you of doing the great things in your life that God wants you to do.

When you activate your faith and allow it to work in your life, you will be amazed at what you are capable of doing. **Remember:** *It is better to do something and fail than to succeed at doing nothing!*

Act today! Even an imperfect effort is better than no effort at all. Direct your action. Determine your path and move forward with conviction.

Fear of not having enough for ourselves keeps us from doing many of the good deeds we could do for others. Once we realize that every good deed reaps a good harvest, we can become a greater "seed spreader." But the *key* is: Don't expect a return on the good deed only from the place you planted it. It very well could come from there, but don't limit God in how He blesses it back to you. Just keep planting good seeds, and God will bless you from sources you may least expect.

> *Nothing in life is to be feared. It is only to be understood.*
> —**Marie Curie**
> **Chemist and physicist**

Of all the quotations I've heard, the one I like least originated with Clare Booth Luce in *H. Faber, The Book of Laws, 1980*: "No good deed goes unpunished." When I hear people quote this it suggests two things to me: First, that the person's act was not freely given, but tht they were expecting something in return for their deed. Second, that they have never seen the beautiful truth that good deeds always bring a blessing, just not necssarily from the person the deed was done for. That's all God's business.

God expects us to be kind and loving toward one another — in fact, He commands it in His Word. He also rewards such acts. Most people find that when they act in kind and loving ways, they are happier. Doing the right things for the right reason — to bring glory to God — *always* comes with its own reward.

It is important to focus on where you are going, and take the necessary actions to get there. But along the way, don't forget to smell the roses, weed the garden of someone who needs you, and share the beauty of the world and yourself with others. One smile given in the morning can multiply by afternoon into enough encouragement for thousands of lives. Some people don't think of smiling as an action, but it is one of the most important gifts of kindness we can share. There is really no telling how far a smile can travel in the span of one day.

When we consistently act with sincere kindness, consideration, respect, and positive enthusiasm, the benefits go far beyond us and our small realm. Our positive actions help determine what kind of world we live in each day. Each act should bring glory to God. It doesn't happen through some hidden or mysterious force. It is something we can see, understand, and influence each time we come into contact with others.

What kind of world would we most like to live in today? This is the question we must answer, and then we must take the necessary actions that will indeed make it happen.

QUESTIONS FOR REFLECTION & DISCUSSION

1. Lou Holtz is quoted as saying, "Ability is what you're capable of doing. Motivation determines what you do. Attitude determines how well you do it." When it comes to accomplishing what you want for your life, this quote seems to pretty well sum it up. But what is missing? Why?

2. If it is true that our actions have the most powerful and dr matic effect on those with whom we come into contact, what should our actions consist of?

3. In the story the author relates about himself and his neighbor, what made the difference in their relationship?
   - How would things have turned out differently if the author had not been willing to submit to his neighbor's unreasonable requests?

4. Romans 8:28 tells us that all things work together for good to those who love God and are called according to his purpose. In the author's story about Shorty Thompson, Thompson was angry with the author for terminating him. Later, though, Thompson thanked the author for doing so. Why?

5. Think about a time in your life when you were at first angry or stressed or disappointed about a circumstance in your life, but it later turned out to be for the best. What would have been the result if things had gone along as you had expected or determined?

6. The author writes: "Attitude is not enough. You must be willing to not only think positively, but live positively as well."
   - In what two ways did he and his family display a positive lifestyle toward their unreasonable neighbor?
   - What was the result of their positive actions?
   - What situation in your life could not only benefit from a positive attitude, but could result in positive changes as a result of your living positively?

7. The author writes, "Act now. Even an imperfect effort is better than no effort at all." What can you do now to positively affect something in your life?
   • If your action does not immediately bring about a positive result, what is the worst thing that can happen?
   • What is the best thing that can happen?
8. Paul tells us in 1 Corinthians 10:31, "Whatsoever you do, do all to the glory of God."
   • Even the smallest act of kindness has a ripple effect. What three things can you do, starting now, to positively affect your life and the lives of others?

POINTS FOR REVIEW:

▶ Attitude is important; actions more so.
▶ Act now.
▶ Even small acts of kindness have a ripple effect.

*You will either step forward
into growth or you will step
back into safety.*

— Abraham Maslow

CHAPTER SIX

Risk Is the Only Way

A ship in harbor is safe,
but that is not what
ships are built for.

— William Shedd

T he late Leo Buscaglia, considered one of the world's foremost producers of personal development materials, including *Personhood: The Art of Being Fully Human* and *Love: What Life Is All About,* wrote:

To hope is to risk pain. To try is to risk failure. But risk must be taken, because the greatest hazard in life is to risk nothing. The person who risks nothing, does nothing, has nothing, is nothing and becomes nothing. He may avoid suffering and sorrow, but he simply cannot learn and feel and change and grow and live and love. Chained by his addictions, he's a slave. He has forfeited his greatest trait, and that is his individual freedom. Only the person who risks is free.

I agree with Buscaglia that only the person who takes risks is really free, but I will go a step further and say you cannot have the success you long for in life unless you are willing to take risks. Far too often, fear rears its ugly head and keeps many people from taking necessary risks, convincing them that if they don't take risks, they can avoid suffering and sorrow. But suffering and sorrow are inevitable — they affect all of us at various times in our lives. Trying to avoid risk does not diminish or lessen those times. In fact, I have seen people actually cause themselves and those they love great suffering and sorrow in their attempts to avoid taking risks.

Taking a risk is the only way to know that we have gone as far we can go with the human resources we have at our disposal. It is only when we take risks that we need to rely on our faith to see us through. My personal belief about risk is based on my faith and built on my knowledge, which tells me that everything in my life is a gift from a great and loving God "who gives generously to all" (James 1:5 NIV). I believe that everything I have now, or will have in the future, comes from Him. He is the supplier of all my needs just as He said He would be and will be for all the days of my life. Therefore, this sincere belief takes some of the sting out of the possibility that someone may take advantage of me or cause me to look like a fool. The fear of loss or appearing to be a fool stops many people from taking some of the most important risks in their lives — those involving great love or great accomplishments.

Why do you think fear is such a prominent topic in the Bible?

Why is so much written about the fact that we are not to fear? And when we allow fear in our lives, where is God in the formula? He isn't in it — it's that simple!

When I think about taking risks, and the awesome possibilities that can result, I am reminded of an incident that occurred at the 2004 Olympic Games in Athens. A young world-class athlete named Paul Hamm gained international fame when he was awarded a gold medal in the overall gymnastic event. Later, the news media had a field day when it was determined that a judge had made a calculation error that had cost the top Korean competitor the gold medal — which supposedly was wrongfully placed around the neck of Paul Hamm. We will never really know the truth of what the actual outcome would have been had the error not occurred. There were many suppositions about how that single calculation could have affected other total scores as well. All we know for sure is that there was a miscalculation and there was no allowance in the rules of the games to remedy this unfortunate happening.

Clouds of Doubt

The news media reported that Paul Hamm was from a small Wisconsin town, and was known for his dream of wanting to become an Olympic gold medal winner. It certainly was not Paul's fault that the miscalculation was made, but as I watched the situation unfold in the news, I saw an incredible opportunity open up for this young man. However, it was an opportunity that involved incredible risk, and I wondered if Paul would be able to recognize it and act on it.

Imagine being in his position, having worked most of your life for the opportunity to compete for an Olympic gold medal. Imagine doing what most young people only dream of doing — arriving at the Olympic Games and competing superbly. Imagine your heart almost beating out of your chest as you stand on the top level of the three-tiered stage, joyfully receiving the gold medal. Imagine the pride of watching the beloved Stars and Stripes being raised as the auditorium is filled with the sound of *your* national anthem.

Then imagine discovering the next day that many people around the world believe the gold medal was awarded to you because of a miscalculation…and that it rightly belongs to a young man from Korea.

This is where Paul Hamm had a beautiful opportunity to risk becoming more than an Olympic gold medal winner. He had already received his medal and proved to the world that he was a deserving athlete, and no one could ever take the honor of that moment away from him. No one would ever forget that. But at that moment, he had the opportunity to take a risk that would have made him a world-class gold medal man of honor.

Very few people in the world have the fortitude, discipline, and courage to become gold medal athletes, but fewer still have the opportunity to win the hearts of the world. I believe that Paul Hamm was given that opportunity. If he had truly realized that no one could ever take the gold medal away from him or erase the fact that the world recognized him as an overall champion, perhaps he could have faced one of the greatest fears known to man — the risk of losing something he so desperately wanted. Had he been willing to give up the medal, I know he would have gained more than he could have ever dreamed. The world would have had an even greater appreciation and respect for him, beyond his athletic prowess. And he would have long been remembered, admired, and loved for his valor in making the concession.

A Missed Opportunity?

As I watched the situation unfold in front of the entire world, I had to wonder what might have happened if Hamm had chosen to risk giving his gold medal to the young Korean athlete who, because of a miscalculation, believed — along with thousands of others — that it had been taken from him.

What Paul Hamm may not have understood is that if he had taken the risk of giving up his medal to someone who had suffered a misfortune, he would have lost nothing, but would have gained so much more — the respect and admiration of the world. He could have become a metaphor for everything that is, and should be, great about sports, the Olympic Games, and human beings in general.

Consider this: When the Olympic Games ended and the September football season rolled around, few people remembered the names of the young athletes who won Olympic gold medals in Athens. Some will likely remember Paul Hamm's name, but how will it be remembered? Now consider the other scenario. Had Hamm taken the risk and given the medal to his fellow athlete who, through no fault of his own, had obviously felt cheated out of his lifelong dream, Hamm would have truly transcended the sport, and instantly become an even larger icon of greatness. He would have been remembered by many — and for all the right reasons. All it takes to make a major difference in society is one great person making a remarkable gesture.

Paul Hamm took many risks on his journey to Athens. The greatest risk was competing against the greatest athletes of the world. I congratulate and applaud the extraordinary risks each great athlete took just to get there. But I wish, for the world's sake as well as for his, that he had considered taking just one more risk — one that truly would have allowed him to become a great example to our society. I believe it would have served him and the world in a magnificent way.

Do you think Paul Hamm's life would be different today had he taken the risk of giving up a gold medal to become a golden example of what a human being can be? I do. And I believe that taking risks is the only sure way for you and me to become all that God wants us to be as well.

Don't be afraid to give up your dream when you are given a great opportunity to fulfill an even greater dream. Consider how much greater Paul Hamm's dream could have been had he made the choice to give up one medal. Where were those who could have helped him to see this? Where are they today in our lives…and would we be willing to listen to them?

Great…or Greater?

Many times in life, we may feel the call of God on our hearts to do a certain thing or to go a certain place — thinking that is our purpose or goal. But often, when we attain what we thought was the ultimate goal, we discover that it was only the beginning of the trip. God's plan may be to get us in motion and then motivate us to go in a different direction. I believe that's why He says in His Word, "A man's mind plans his way, but the Lord directs his steps and makes them sure" (Proverbs 16:9 AMP).

I believe it is wise to have a plan, because people without

a plan are often tempted to do nothing. But as we follow our plan, we must be willing to set it aside if God leads us in another direction. There is a fine balance in working our plan, while trusting God to lead us through His *perfect* plan.

God wants to impact our lives, but we must be willing to let go of our own plans in favor of His. And it is almost always a guarantee that what He calls us to do, we won't be able to do in our own power. It most likely will require faith. How many times has Satan robbed you of your faith by filling you with fear? The Bible says we can't please God without faith, so we must trust Him enough to follow His direction. We should never be afraid to follow God's plan instead of our own, because He always leads us to what is best for us.

Let me illustrate by way of an example. Suppose that one day I sense that God is compelling me to drive to Dallas for a particular reason. Then on the way to Dallas, I have a distinct feeling and belief that He wants me to change direction and go to Fort Smith, Arkansas. Since God knows all things, including His purpose for our lives, we find far greater joy and excitement in this life when we just live our lives walking out his plan, as we will and are doing, knowing that He truly is leading and guiding each step of he way, just as He says in His Word. I must have faith in Him and trust His plan, believing that He has a purpose for me in Fort Smith. Perhaps I am to be a lifeline to someone there who is in desperate need.

One might ask, "Then why would God have first caused you to believe He was leading you to go to Dallas?" Only God knows for sure, but it could be that I might not have been open to hearing Him say, "Go to Fort Smith." But once I was on the trip, I was open to hearing the call to Fort Smith.

When Proverbs 16:9 tells us "a man's mind plans his way, but the Lord directs his steps and makes them sure" (AMP), it means it's okay to have plans, but we need to keep foremost in our minds that God will change those plans as He deems appropriate. He is truly in control of our lives.

Fear says you need to know and understand everything before you take action, but faith says when you know the Master of the universe, it is safe to move out in complete trust. Isaiah 30:21 tells us: "If you leave God's paths and go astray, you will hear a voice behind you say, 'No, this is the way; walk here'" (TLB).

We don't know God's master plan or how He may want to use us to fulfill that plan — and our human reasoning may cause us to have doubts or even fear. But if we truly trust God, He can calm those fears as we obediently step out in faith and follow the leading of His still small voice.

> You are the only person on earth who can use your ability.
>
> — Zig Ziglar

Every experience, every risk, every effort is an investment that can result in bettering who we are as human beings. We can either invest in making our life and the lives of others better by what we do, or, through complacency or fear, settle for less than our God-given potential. It is my desire, purpose, and privilege to use my talents, resources, and actions, to better my community and the world as a whole. I believe this is only possible as I am willing to take the necessary risks along the way.

It Is Not a Risk If It's God's Plan

When I ran for governor of Oklahoma as an Independent candidate in 2002, was that a risk? It all depends on how you look at it.

In any political campaign, there is always the potential that a candidate's reputation may be called into question. I had a very good reputation — and, hopefully, still do — with regard to being somewhat politically astute, and yet I was running as an Independent, which is considered to be "way out in left field." Another consideration that had to be acknowledged and accepted was the risk of the financial burden that was involved. The only way I could do that was to put my total trust in God. I knew He had led me to run in the race, and I also knew that where God guides, He provides. So I knew He would provide for all my needs. I ended up spending close to $2.3 million on a campaign I didn't win — but God hasn't let me down yet!

I took the position — as I have for many years, and still do — that there really is no risk when we feel that God is leading us to do a certain thing. Yet in the eyes of man, running for governor was a great risk. Some may wonder why anyone would step out of his "comfort zone" for something that appears to be such a risk. For me it was a matter of following what I felt was God's plan for my life. I felt that I could make a meaningful difference to the people of Oklahoma as their governor. Sometimes, fulfilling our potential requires stepping "outside of the box." Only history will tell the complete story. One that God knew before the foundations of the earth.

Fulfilling the Call

When I had surgery in California to correct a serious sleep apnea problem, I met another man who is of the same mind. The surgeon, Dr. Nelson Powell, is a world-renowned physician, best known for his sleep apnea surgical procedures. As Dr. Powell and I visited and shared about our professions, I learned that when he began pursuing the possibility of doing the sleep apnea procedure, his peers strongly discouraged him. Since he was enjoying a comfortable and lucrative practice, they wondered why he would risk destroying his reputation as a fine surgeon.

I understood. I told him that I knew he had made the choice because he was more concerned about helping people than the possibility of hurting his own image and reputation — that he was willing to take a chance in order to help people like me who had a life-threatening problem. He assured me that I was right, and we discussed the similarities of our convictions about taking risks in order to help people and fulfill our callings.

I believe I have the calling of God on my life, and fulfilling that call to give of myself to help other people, however He chooses, is worth any "risk" that may be involved. My faith

> You have to find something that you love enough to be able to take risks, jump over the hurdles and break through the brick walls that are always going to be placed in front of you. If you don't have that kind of feeling for what it is you're doing, you'll stop at the first giant hurdle.
>
> — George Lucas

in His good plan for my life far exceeds any fear or concern about harming my image or reputation.

I find it interesting that twice since the 2002 election, I have been courted by some of the leaders of the Republican party to run for governor again. I made such a positive showing as an Independent in 2002 by getting 76 percent of the swing vote, that they have asked me to consider running again — as a Republican.

The bottom line seems to be that not only did I not damage my image and reputation — I "enhanced" them. The beauty of it is that my purpose for running had nothing to do with damaging or enhancing my reputation...and everything to do with following God's plan for my life.

Risk or Run?

When my oldest son, Chuck — who is now the managing partner of our law firm — was a freshman at Baylor University, he called me one night; it was obvious that he was distressed. After giving me his anxious and lengthy explanation, he finally got around to telling me the purpose of his call. He wanted to talk me into giving him permission to drop out of the finite math class he was taking. He explained that he just couldn't do the work because it was so difficult. He argued that he hadn't received a good math background in high school, and that most of the other students in this math class were upperclassmen. He couldn't understand why the university counselor had suggested this class for him. I could hear the confusion and panic in his voice, so I suggested that we meet in Dallas the upcoming Thursday evening to discuss the matter more fully. He was relieved at my suggestion, telling me that he had a test coming up the following week and needed to make a decision as quickly as possible.

When we met in Dallas on Thursday evening, I began our conversation by telling Chuck that he was never again to insult his intelligence, his mother's, nor mine, by saying/ believing that this math course was an intellectual impossibility for him. I felt that I needed to make the point that it wasn't an issue of *could* or *couldn't*, but whether or not he was willing to *pay the price*. I let him know I understood that the class was more challenging for him because he did not have the high school math background he needed. But I assured him that successfully completing this course was not an impossibility for him. I pointed out that he might have to study as many as fifty or sixty hours to pass the same test that would require maybe ten or fifteen hours of study for the better-prepared students. And I assured him that he *could* do it. I further explained that life, in my opinion, was about choosing which risks we were willing to take, and that we should never allow fear to keep us from taking them.

I mentioned that each of us, at one time or another, must choose to overcome fear and risk facing challenges, and that the only way to do that is by allowing our God-given knowledge and wisdom to see us through. I explained that the only other option is to allow fear to make us run from our challenges, and that once we start, it becomes easier and easier to run...and it's never fulfilling. I told Chuck that he must choose how he would prefer to live his life, reminding him that deciding whether he would "risk or run" from his challenges was one of the privileges and pressures that came with being an adult.

I assured him that I would support his decision, even if he chose to discontinue the course — or even college, for that matter — but that I hoped for his sake he would take this decision very seriously.

Chuck decided to take the risk, stay in the class, and take the upcoming test. He not only took the test the following week, but he made the top grade in the class! He set the curve.

Chuck's story is used as an example in a book written by Paul Meyers of Success Motivation International.

Too many men and women forsake their dreams, gifts, talents, and heart's desires because fear keeps them from being willing to take the risk. Most are afraid that they are not up to the challenge...or they are not sure that their dreams are good enough, or that they are good enough to accomplish them. Too often, this is simply an excuse to let fear, instead of faith, rule their lives. Remember, fear doesn't just come on us — we choose it.

> *The greatest mistake a man can make is to be afraid of making one.*
>
> **— Elbert Hubbard**

What about you? Are you willing to face your fears and take risks in order to accomplish your dreams? If you had permission to do what you really wanted to do, and you knew that you could not fail, what would you do? Most people don't ask this question of themselves because they are afraid to even risk the answer. Fear of failure causes them to ask, "How am I going to pull it off?" The answer is simple: You take consistent, small steps in the direction of your dreams. If you spend all your energy avoiding the possibility of failure, then failure becomes your focus and your most obvious possibility — the ruler of your life. No one dreams of failing, and yet many, simply by attempting to avoid it, accomplish just that...and it becomes their life's greatest accomplishment.

Talk to those you know who have had great success in life, and you will always find that when fear tried to rule them, they looked it squarely in the face and said *No*. They chose faith.

Embrace Life's Risks

To win at the game of life, you must be willing to embrace life's risks. I am not talking about taking foolish risks. That would be foolhardy. Of course, we have to be discerning about the kind of risks we are willing to take. But it is even more foolish to completely avoid taking risks of any kind than to occasionally take a risk in life and fail.

> *Risks don't always turn out as we hoped, but they always bring greater insight and reward of living every day to the fullest.*
>
> **— Mary Kay Mueller**

If you decide not to take a risk, never let it be because of fear. Let it be because of knowledge and wisdom. Remember the illustration of the snake in chapter one, and the fact we established — that it is not fear that motivates us to move to safety, but knowledge and wisdom. When you really see this principle, you will never again see fear as your friend. Rather, you will see knowledge and wisdom as your friend and fear as the great destroyer.

When you choose to live your life to the fullest — when you are ready to really live, take action, and be self-responsible — there is always a chance that things won't turn out the way you had hoped. So what? Without taking action, you are sure to never accomplish anything, so where is the real risk? Every time you make a decision, there is a chance that you could be wrong. However, the flip side is that if you never make a decision, you can never get anything right. So the real risk is in not taking a risk; and a fear-based life causes the problem. Consider your life and your ability to take risks, and ask yourself if God is included in your formula. He is a necessary and important part of the equation.

It is in our willingness to take risks that our ultimate opportunities lay. I agree that it is important to know the risks involved in moving in a particular direction. I agree that you need to prepare for risks, manage them, and acclimate yourself to living with them. But only when you are willing to live with the possibility of failure, are you truly on your way to achieving amazing success. There are no guarantees in this life. There are only risks. But it is your willingness to break through the barriers imposed by risk that enables you to make your dream a reality. People who avoid taking risks spend their lives wondering, "What if…?"

What worries you, masters you.
— Haddon W. Robinson

The Bible tells us to "be anxious for nothing" (Philippians 4:6). This is a powerful spiritual *directive*. This, to me, seems to be a request, not just a suggestion. Do you agree? In a very practical sense, this instruction allows us to believe in ourselves and in the purpose God puts in our hearts. It also assures us of the support we need to take the necessary risks that will make a meaningful difference in our lives.

Some people believe that God is some far-off deity or a stern judge; but consider, if you will, that He is a beneficent force. He is obvious in nature — the life principle that makes the flowers bud and the plants grow, and He spreads abundance about us with a lavish hand. He is the universal mind that holds all supply. He knows the desires of every heart, gives us our childhood dreams, and fulfills our need of maturity. And don't ever forget this: God often uses our failures to bring maturity. All that we need in order to obtain our heart's desire from God is a right understanding of His availability, realizing that *nothing can happen in our lives except the things that He allows.* Once we understand God's love — truly understand it — we will no longer see fear as our friend; we will be anxious for nothing, and we will shed our sense of limitation, just as Chuck did in his math course.

The "fear nots" found throughout the Bible, from beginning to end, are really instructions on how to accomplish the challenging tasks that are likely to find their way into our path. The Bible clearly tells us that we are to trust God. When fear tries to overtake us, we can look it in the face and combat it with faith. Confess the words of Psalm 56:3 TLB: "When I am afraid, I will put my confidence in you. Yes, I will trust the promises of God." That kind of faith will look fear in the face, overcome it, and touch the very heart of God.

In Deuteronomy 6:5 NASB, we read these instructions: "You shall love the Lord your God with all your heart and with all your soul and with all your might." Above all, God wants us to love Him and trust Him, and we cannot do that if we give our hearts to fear instead of to Him. God will not join us in a formula of fear, but He will show us a better way when we have faith enough to ask for and trust in His help.

"Faith is the substance of things hoped for, the evidence of things not seen" (Hebrews 11:1). Most of us know this verse of scripture in our head, but how many of us know it in our heart? As a child, I had a lot of fear. I can look back today and see how God used that to help develop me. My parents frequently encouraged me, assuring me that things would work out for my ultimate good, even if they seemed extremely challenging at times. My parents instilled in me a sense of faith that has allowed me to move through my life with a higher degree of confidence and security than many people I have met.

Faith — the Foundation of Success

Faith is the foundation of success. It is what holds up our hopes and dreams, and it comes by knowledge. Most people have faith; but the important question is "faith in what?" You can either have faith that things will work out for your good, or that life will work out according to your fears. Read and study God's Word, gaining knowledge, and your faith will be strengthened so you can overcome fear — which you know by now is not your friend.

I'm sure you have heard people say things like, "Nothing good ever happens in my life," "People always take advantage of me," "I can never get a break," "I can't find a fulfill-ing relationship," "I can't find a decent job," or "I just have bad luck." Did you know these are all faith statements? When people make these statements, they don't understand that they are expressing their sadly misplaced faith. They have turned their hearts and lives over to the futility of fear. What a waste of the most powerful gift we possess — the gift of faith.

If you have an underlying belief that nothing good ever happens to you, then guess what? Nothing good ever happens to you! Why? Because that is your picture of life. The thing you put your faith in — the thing you believe — is what you will get. So it is reasonable to assume that if you have faith in fear, you cannot simultaneously have faith in God. He will not be in that formula you have put together. Fear and faith cannot coexist. Typically, we create it, and then we get what we expect. Expect the worst, and you will probably predict with great accuracy what will happen to you.

> There is no philosophy by which a man can do a thing when he thinks he can't. The reason why millions of men are plodding along in mediocrity today, many of them barely making a living when they have the ability to do something infinitely bigger, is because they lack confidence in themselves.
>
> — Robert Collier
> Secret of the Ages

Spiritually speaking, faith is confidence in the knowl-edge that God is who He says He is, and that He will do what He has promised to do. Faith is not a power of force. It is not a vehicle by which we can coerce God into something against His will. It is simply an expression of confidence in the person and character of God. It is the proper response to the promise or revelation of God.

True faith is like God walking with you, whispering in your ear, and holding your hand through every part of your day. It is a peace like no other — a peace that comes from deep within. It's the only real security. Any other sense of security is an illusion. Faith is the starting point for joy. It is resting in His sureness that allows us to live without fear or worry. We must really "get" this concept in order to see that fear is never our friend!

God makes no mistakes. He has created within each of us a purpose — a work for us to do that will fulfill our lives and bring glory to Him. When we are attempting to live our purpose and move in the direction of our dreams, we are vulnerable to confusion. Fear confuses many people, paralyzing them and rendering them incapable of making good choices for their lives.

Some people will advise: "Don't worry about your purpose. Go where the money is." In fact, that might sum up the attitude of the vast majority of truly fearful people. Why do they make this kind of recommendation? Because most people are afraid and don't want to be. They mistakenly believe that money is the answer to eliminating the fear they don't want in their lives. They don't understand that fear is merely a creative thought in negative form.

Robert Collier, in his book *Secret of the Ages*, tells us, "We sometimes cry out that we are driven by force or circumstances. Yet the fact remains that we do those things which we choose to do, for even though we may not wish to go a certain way, we allow ourselves to pursue it because it offers the least resistance."

Many of us make major decisions in our lives based on fear. Fear suggests that we take the path that requires the least of us. If fear is the motivating factor behind an important decision, we can rest assured that it is not the decision God would have us make for our lives, and He won't be a part of that formula. God is an abundant God, and He has more for us than we can imagine for ourselves. He did not create man, or anything else that exists in the world, out of limitation. We are not designed to live in fear of lack. God created us in His image, and His image is miraculous and abundant. Therefore, real abundance can only be found if we follow the direction that He intends for our lives.

Many people don't understand God's abundance and His desire to supply it to His children. I was once asked to join a friend in praying that God would meet the need of an evangelist who was to be preaching in an upcoming revival. When I asked why we should do that, he seemed confused. Then I said, "Why would we bother God with a request that He has already promised to supply? He says in His Word, 'My God shall supply all your needs according to His riches in glory...'" (Philippians 4:19 NASB). That sounds like a "done deal" to me. I think the problem is that we often get confused about a *need* versus a *want.*

Too many today are far too focused on getting and having, earning and spending, with little thought of how God wants them to use the resources He provides for them. We are told in Matthew 6:33 to "seek first the kingdom of God and His righteousness, and all these things shall be added to you" (NKJV).

Jim Elliot, a martyred missionary in South America, made an entry in his diary that should bring new perspective about the divine plan for our finances. He wrote: ***He is no fool who gives what he cannot keep to gain what he cannot lose.***

Moving in Faith

Back in the '70s, at the age of thirty-three, I left my job in Houston as sales manager for an insurance company, where I was making in excess of $60,000 a year. I had a company car, an expense account, and was doing well, but I made the decision to accept the position of assistant insurance commissioner in my home state of Oklahoma, which paid $12,500 a year, without a car or expense account.

Pessimists calculate the odds. Optimists believe they can overcome them.
— Ted Koppel

"Why in the world would you do a stupid, risky thing like that?" my friends and associates asked. "What! You're taking a new job that will pay you less...much less?" Most of my friends believed that I had lost my mind. I never subscribed to that conditioning. I had three children, and I didn't know how I could possibly make it, but I knew that God had moved on my heart to go. I put my trust in God, and went where I believed He was leading me to go. I chose my faith to guide me, instead of letting fear intimidate and limit me.

My wife's reaction to my decision confirmed that I was following God's leading. When I told her about my decision, she wasn't surprised. God had already prepared her by giving her a kind of "knowing" about the upcoming move to Oklahoma City. The amazing and beautiful thing about her reaction is the fact that she completely trusted my walk with God. And even though I was taking a job that paid just 25 percent of what I was making, she wasn't concerned about it. She had witnessed the faithfulness of God in our lives in the past, and she had no fear about the future. That's quite a testimony to the importance of a man being the godly head of his home. When a man faithfully follows the leading of God, it brings great security to his wife — even when it means a 75 percent cut in income!

I can tell you that God honored our faith and obedience, and provided for our every need from His abundant storehouse. You can't lose when you follow God's plan.

According to John Eldredge in his book *Wild at Heart:*

Don't ask how, that will cut your desire off at the knees. *How* is never the right question, how is a faithless question. It means "unless I can see my way clearly I won't believe it, won't venture forth." *How* is God's department. He is asking you *what.* What is written in your heart? What makes you come alive? If you could do what you've always wanted to do, what would it be? You see, a man's calling is written on his true heart, and he discovers it when he enters the frontier of his deep desires. To paraphrase [religious anthropologist Gil] Bailie, don't ask yourself what the world needs, ask yourself what makes you come alive because what the world needs are *men* who have come alive.

The only way to live life as the rich adventure it is — with all its danger, unpredictability, and uncertainty — is in an intimate and ongoing relationship with God. He is the source of all greatness, and certainly the only thing in life worth the reverence that we too often give to fear. The control we crave is an illusion. According to Oswald Chambers, in his book *My Utmost for His Highest:*

> Naturally, we are inclined to be so mathematical and calculating that we look upon uncertainty as a bad thing….Certainty is the mark of the commonsense life, gracious uncertainty is the mark of the spiritual life. To be certain of God means that we are uncertain of all our ways, we do not know what a day may bring forth. This is generally said with a sigh of sadness, it should rather be an expression of breathless expectation.

Leap with Both Feet!

When it comes to loving, giving, growing, and making a difference in the world, you must be willing to leap with both feet off your personal cliff of limitations. Leap with faith toward something that you dream, and away from that which you fear. This is what my dad meant that night on the porch, when in his eyes I could see the message, "Fear is never our friend." Fear tells you there is a way to be safe in this world, a way to not risk yourself; but life insists — as does God — that you will only find the peace, joy, hope, happiness, and success that you desire when you are willing, with faith, to risk who you are at this moment for who God would have you become.

If you have never read "The Dash" by Linda M. Ellis, you should do so. In this poem, the dash refers to the line representing all the time between someone's date of birth and date of death. The poem reminds us that how we spend the dash is what matters most of all — not the material possessions we accumulate along the way, but the way we live our lives and treat other people. It concludes by asking if you would be proud of the things that are said about how you spent your dash.

In an online interview, Ellis summarized the poem as saying, "You never know how long your dash will be, so make every day count."

Too often in our lives the only dash we care about is the one to lunch, to the bank, to school, or to the game. What changes would you have to make in the way you live your life in order for the people who attend your funeral to make the statement, "_____(write your name here)_____was a person of great faith, who lived a fearless life."

Is it even possible to live a fearless life? Is there really such a place, a place where fear finds no soil in which to take root? I believe there is!

In the next chapter, you will discover where you can find such a place.

Questions for Reflection & Discussion

1. "A ship in harbor is safe, but that is not what ships are built for."
    *   What did William Shedd mean by this statement?
2. Webster defines the word *risk* as "the possibility of suffering harm or loss: danger."
    *   What sort of danger is involved in taking a risk?
    *   Why?
3. 'To hope is to risk pain," Leo Buscaglia tells us. "To try is to risk failure. But risk must be taken, because the greatest hazard in life is to risk nothing."
    *   What is the hazard in *not* taking a risk?
    *   Why is success in life not possible without risks?
4. Philippians 4:19 tells us, "My God shall supply all your need according to his riches in glory by Christ Jesus."
    *   If you can be assured that God will always supply your needs, does that help remove the fear of taking a risk?
    *   Why or why not?
5. Risk involves power. What power do you suddenly possess when you are willing to take a risk?
6. The author relates a story about Paul Hamm, the young American, who, during the 2004 Olympic Games, gained international fame when he was awarded the gold medal in the overall gymnastic event. Later it was determined that the judges had made an error in calculating the score and the medal should have gone to the Korean gymnast.
    *   How could Paul Hamm have risked being more than an Olympic gold medalist?
    *   How would have taking that risk changed his life?
    *   Why do you think he chose not to take that risk?
    *   What do you think you would have done?
7. Why does the author use the term "investment" to describe every experience, every risk, every effort in our lives?

8. What are the "dividends" that can be derived from such investments?

9. How can you use your own experiences, efforts and risks to better yourself and those around you?

10. If you are not willing to take a risk, what are you giving up?

11. If you are willing to take a risk, how does that change your options in life?

12. In the story the author related about his son's fear of not being able to succeed in his finite math class in college, the author explained to his son that it was not a matter of whether he could or couldn't succeed in that class, but whether he was willing to pay the price to succeed.

    • Is there a fear in your life that is keeping you from being willing to pay the price to succeed in an area of your life?

    • If so, what steps must you take to overcome that fear and be willing to pay the price for success?

13. If you had permission to do what you really wanted to do, and you knew you could not fail, what would you do?

14. If you spend all of your energy avoiding the possibility of failure, failure becomes your most obvious possibility.

    • Do you agree with the above statement?

    • Why or why not?

POINTS FOR REVIEW

▶ He who shrinks from risk is left to spend life wondering what could have been.

▶ The greatest hazard in life is to risk nothing.

▶ Risk is the only sure way to become all that God has in store for you.

Fear is the soil
where faith grows!

— Author Unknown

CHAPTER SEVEN

NO FEAR —
Is There Such a Place?

The remarkable thing about fearing God is that
when you fear God, you fear nothing else, whereas
if you do not fear God, you fear everything else.

— Oswald Chambers

I am sure that you, like many others today, wonder if there really is a place where we can find freedom from fear. Think about this a minute. Would God admonish, instruct, and encourage us to "be anxious for nothing" (Philippians 4:6 NKJV) if there were no such place...or if it were impossible to find it? The Bible provides the answer in Numbers 23:19, where it clearly states, "God is not a man, that he should lie" (NIV).

God, our loving Father, would never tell us about a place where there is no fear if it didn't exist or if it were impossible to find and attain it. We are His children; He loves us and wants us to enjoy all the benefits He has made available to us, including freedom from fear. But we cannot find this wonderful place on our own — we must include God in the process. We must read His Word to acquire the necessary knowledge and instructions, and we must pray and ask God to help us. There *is* a place where you can be free from fear, and God wants to help you find it.

You may also wonder about what the Bible refers to as "the fear of God." There is an amazing connection here that I will discuss in this final chapter.

I knew when I wrote this book that the one argument I might encounter was, "What about the scriptures that tell us to fear God? How can you say that fear is never our friend, when the Bible tells us that we are to fear God?" This is a very important question — one that I have thoroughly researched and discussed with a number of Bible scholars, especially in recent years as I prepared to write this book.

As we contemplate the word *fear* as it applies to the "fear of God," we find that it does not mean dread, or apprehension, but rather awe, reverence, and the highest respect for the One who created us and loves us. This is a spiritual fear, not an earthly fear. It is a profound sense of veneration, honor, and respect that enables us to truly worship and adore God — to develop a true, complete, and wonderful devotion toward Him. It is impossible to be truly devoted and dedicated to God without developing a profound sense of reverence and awe of Him. It is through eyes of reverence that we first see God in His transcendent glory, majesty, and holiness. Through these same eyes of reverence, we see His presence in the miracle of a newborn baby, or in the glorious evening sky, the majesty of the mountains, or the beauty of the ocean.

We must understand the meaning of reverence before we can truly appreciate God's infinite love, mercy, grace, and power. Even though man was created in the image of God, there is an infinite gap between the worth and dignity of God the Creator, and His creation. As we witness the greatness of all that He has created, we must remember that we are but pieces of the magnificent puzzle. He is the One who shaped and formed every piece.

The fear of God is not fear, in the sense that man feels fear — it is not dread or anxiety. It does not de-motivate us; it motivates us. It is heartfelt humility born out of the recognition of this vast difference between God and man. It is not a "put down" of man but, instead, it's the opposite. It is the "exaltation of God," the result of which gives man his worth.

When we surrender to and embrace our relationship with God, we begin to learn the true meaning of respect, adoration, and admiration of His holy attributes. When we truly have the "fear of God," it is evidenced in the reverence, awe, love, and respect that we have for Him.

It is easy to see then, that "the fear of God" is nothing like the other fears we experience in life. If you ran a reference search on all the scriptures that refer to "the fear of God," you would quickly recognize that it is, in fact, a very beneficial fear. Here are just a few.

The Fear of the Lord...

...prolongeth days (Proverbs 10:27).

...is a fountain of life (Proverbs 14:27).

...is strong confidence: and his children shall have a place of refuge (Proverbs 14:26).

…is the beginning of wisdom: a good understanding have all
they that do his commandments… (Psalm 111:10).

Notice that the last scripture speaks about wisdom. This
is important information because wisdom, the knowledge
of truth, will dilute all our debilitating fears and give us
confidence.

Our conviction and faith in God's holy and gracious
attributes allow us to be at peace and resist the life-stealing,
destructive fear that lives on earth. First John 4:18 tells us
that perfect love casts out fear — that is, our love, our fear
of God, cancels out all other fears that knock at our heart's
door, trying to invade our privacy and force their ugly selves
into our lives. Our love, trust, and fear of God will help us
live in such a way that when fear knocks, faith locks it out.

Oswald Chambers expresses this truth so well in the
quotation at the beginning of this chapter. Read it again and
allow the words to sink into your heart. Take a moment to
reflect on the simplicity and truth of the message.

Fear God and Find Freedom

When we "fear the Lord," the promises in His Word
become even more meaningful to us. We discover that the
truth of His Word gives us new confidence and brings new
freedom to our lives.

Psalm 27:2-3 tells us, "When the wicked, even mine
enemies and my foes, came upon me to eat my flesh, they
stumbled and fell. Though an host should encamp against
me, my heart shall not fear: though war should rise against
me, in this will I be confident."

We can confidently confess with the psalmist that our heart will know no fear. And when we do, the world is stripped of its power over us. We are free. We may be faced with all kinds of wars, but with our confidence and trust in the Lord, we will be *victorious.*

The psalmist goes on to say, "In the time of trouble he shall hide me in his pavilion: in the secret of his tabernacle shall he hide me; he shall set me upon a rock" (Psalm 27:5). Now, that sounds like a fear-free atmosphere... and it is ours!

When fear tries to creep into our minds and hearts, we can find freedom in God's Word, which says:

- "Don't be afraid, for I am with you. Do not be dismayed, for I am your God. I will strengthen you. I will help you. I will uphold you with my victorious right hand" (Isaiah 41:10 NLT).

- "I am leaving you with a gift — peace of mind and heart. And the peace I give isn't like the peace the world gives. So don't be troubled or afraid" (John 14:27 NLT).

- "Don't worry about anything; instead, pray about everything; tell God your needs and don't forget to thank him for his answers. If you do this you will experience God's peace, which is far more wonderful than the human mind can understand. His peace will keep your thoughts and your hearts quiet and at rest as you trust in Christ Jesus" (Philippians 4:6-7 TLB).

The knowledge of God's Word is our friend, and without it we cannot find that place of "no fear."

When we choose to take God at His Word and believe His promises, we will not allow any external happening to grieve or frighten us. We will be confident that external things are but passing shadows of no permanent importance. Hidden in the secret place of His tabernacle, nothing can harm us. We are like a house set upon a rock that is safe and secure in the midst of the storms. (See Matthew 7:24.)

It Is All About Him

In this world of political correctness — a world in which we are careful not to offend anyone — too often we risk watering down who we are called to be in the sight of God. We hear much about God's love today, His faithfulness, and His favor; but what about our faithfulness, our love, and our favor that should be His and His alone? Could it be that in our attempt to be all-encompassing and inviting to others we are not spending an adequate amount of time focusing on the reverent fear and respect that it is our privilege and responsibility to pay to God?

His love for us is the highest and greatest love that exists. We must be careful not to magnify our perception of God's love in a way that we, as spoiled children, begin to believe that it is His responsibility to love us instead of recognizing that it is our responsibility and privilege to focus on loving Him. This twisted, entitled perspective on the greatest love that exists can cause us to believe that God's love is about us and our worthiness, instead of about *Him* and His ultimate grace.

We cannot fully appreciate God's love until we study His Word and understand His infinite majesty. He created us for *His* glory, not ours.

Only with a reverent fear of God can we truly begin to understand and appreciate the immense love that He has for us. He is aware of the infinite gulf between himself and His creation, but out of His ultimate grace and mercy He chooses to love us without fail. God's love for us is multifaceted.

> Let all the earth fear the Lord; let all the inhabitants of the world stand in awe.
> — Psalm 33:8

Evidence of it surrounds us every day. But His most supreme demonstration to date is that He sent His Son to die for our sins. Can there be any greater love? For that ultimate gift — which would have been more than sufficient — and a million others, it is imperative that we begin to understand how much God, and only God, deserves our focus, our dedication, our complete reverence, respect, and spiritual fear.

Let us be inspired by the everyday miracles we witness to open our hearts, reflect on His great love for us, and then pray, "Oh, Lord, let me reach these heights in my worship today — unlimited respect, adoration, admiration, and a concentrated focus on You. May this worship create within me a breathless, reverent silence in which I can hear Your voice and heed Your direction for my life. Let me experience that 'reverential fear' of You today so that, in my heart, there is room for no other. Amen."

When we understand the powerful consequences of our willingness to surrender completely to God, we free ourselves of the world's power to cause us anxiety.

In Emmet Fox's daily devotional book *Around the Year with Emmet Fox*, the devotional for September 30 reads as follows:

Cut My Own Throat

A man came to see me in London in great distress. He had attended some lectures I had given, and wanted advice. He was the owner of a general grocery store in a village in the south of England, and hitherto there had been no competition. Now, one of the big chain stores was opening a branch almost opposite to him in the main street, and he was in a panic.

He said, "How can I compete with them? I am ruined."

I said, "You know the Great Law. You know where your supply comes from. Why be afraid?"

He said, "*I Must Do Something.*"

I said, "Stand in your shop each morning and bless it, by claiming that divine Power works through it for great prosperity and peace for all concerned." He nodded his head in agreement.

I added, "Then look down the street to where they are fitting up the new store, and bless that in the same way."

"What? Cut my own throat?" he almost screamed.

I explained that what blesses one, blesses

all. I told him that he was really hating his competitor *through fear* and that his hatred would destroy him, while blessing the "enemy" was the way to get rid of hate. I finished by saying, "You cannot cut your throat with prayer, you can only improve everything."

It took some time to persuade him, but at last he got the idea, and when I met him several years later he told me that his business had been better than ever since the chain store appeared; and that it seemed to be getting on well too.

This is a good example of what Jesus meant when He said, "Love your enemies" (Luke 6:27). Love and fear cannot coexist. When we are dedicated to trusting God and blessing those whom we fear instead of hating them through fear, we open up God's unlimited resources to do His will in our lives. Will we like everything that happens in our lives? No. God may not intend for us to like everything that happens in our lives, but He does intend to use it for our good, to make us more like Him. Once we are convinced of His love for us and believe that He has a good plan for our lives, we have no further need for fear. It becomes irrelevant in our lives, and we see it as the sad and pathetic thief that it is.

First John 4:18 tells us that perfect love casts out fear. But we cannot love perfectly; only God can. It is through our faith and trust in Him and in His plan for our lives, that our fear is banished.

"How can I grow my faith?" many have asked me. I hope this book has helped answer that question. You grow your faith by strengthening it, through the knowledge of God's Word, and exercising it every day. You grow your faith by choosing it over and over again. It takes focus and discipline, but more importantly, it takes desire.

If you truly desire to increase your faith, you must invest your efforts, your discipline, and your heart in the only thing that really matters — your faith in God. Get to know Him just as you get to know your earthly father. Spend time with Him. You can honor Him by trusting the life He has given you to His care, knowing that the plan He has for you is better than any plan you could possibly have for yourself.

> How long should you try?
> Until.
>
> — Jim Rohn

Again, His plan will require an investment of time and commitment on your part — I can't emphasize this enough. You must be willing to study His Word and spend time in prayer and meditation. Mark 11:24 says, "Therefore I tell you, whatever you ask for in prayer, believe that you have received it, and it will be yours" (NIV). The resources of God are made available to us through prayer.

As you give yourself to gaining more knowledge about God's Word and His plan for your life, and seeking His will, He will give you the desires of your heart. As your faith grows, you will find that you are willing to risk doing whatever God asks of you, and His purpose for your life will be accomplished.

Invest your efforts, your discipline, and your heart into the only thing that really matters — your faith in God. Give the life that He gave you back to Him and trust that the plan

He has for you is better than any plan you have for yourself. Be willing to risk what He calls you to risk, and be what He calls you to be. Don't insist on knowing all the details — just put your trust in the One who is your source, the Alpha and Omega.

How do you get to the place where fear no longer exists? You make one faithful choice at a time, and at each fork in the road of your life, each turn on your path, you choose faith over and over again.

> *I will persist until I succeed. Always will I take another step. If that is of no avail, I will take another, and yet another. In truth, one step at a time is not too difficult... I know that small attempts, repeated, will complete any undertaking.*
>
> **— Og Mandino**

There is no sudden leap to greatness in faith or in life. Success comes from doing, day by day, again and again, that which you believe will take you where your heart desires to be. Remember that what you give your efforts, your heart, your time, and your energy to will build value far into the future, and will bring with it a fulfillment that lasts. Make a wise investment by living a fearless life. Life is filled with twenty-four hours a day — no more, no less — and only you can choose how to invest that time.

Faithfulness equals fearlessness. I recommend that you choose to live a fearless life. I encourage you to create outcomes for your life that will make a difference and bring you peace and joy. Spend your time and efforts in ways that will leave the world a better place long after you are gone.

God bless you as you choose a life of fearlessness. I pray that the evidence I have presented here has convinced you to agree: *Fear is* **never** *our friend!*

A Final Note

When the Wind Blows

A young man applied for a job as a farm hand. When the farmer asked for his qualifications, he said, "I can sleep when the wind blows." This puzzled the farmer. But he liked the young man, and hired him. A few days later, the farmer and his wife were awakened in the night by a violent storm.

They quickly began to check things out to see if all was secure. They found that the shutters of the farmhouse had been securely fastened. A good supply of logs had been set next to the fireplace.

The young man slept soundly.

The farmer and his wife then inspected their property. They found that the farm tools had been placed in the storage shed, safe from the elements. The tractor had been moved into the garage. The barn was properly locked. Even the animals were calm. All was well. The farmer then understood the meaning of the young man's words, "I can sleep when the wind blows." Because the farmhand did his work loyally and faithfully when the skies were clear, he was prepared for the storm when it broke. So when the wind blew, he was not afraid. He could sleep in peace.

— Author Unknown

Questions for Reflection & Discussion

1. What does it mean to fear God?

2. How does this differ from the kind of fear we are not to have?

3. What must we truly understand about God before we can appreciate His love, mercy, grace and ultimate beneficent power?

4. What happens to us when we surrender to, and embrace, our relationship with God?

5. What allows us to be at peace and resist the life-stealing, destructive fear that can overtake our hearts?

6. The author says in today's politically-correct world — a world where we are careful not to offend — we risk watering down who we are called to be in the sight of God. Who exactly are we called to be and why?

7. How should knowing who we are called to be change the way we think about ourselves and our place in this world?

8. Knowing this then, why is it imperative that we understand how much God, and only God, deserves our focus, our dedication, our complete reverence, respect and our spiritual fear?

9. How will this change the way we view ourselves, the circumstances in our lives, and those around us?

10. This chapter relates a story by Emmet Fox about a businessman who feared competition from a much bigger competitor. To this man's horror, Mr. Fox advised the man to pray for his competitor. After much doubt at such a suggestion, the man took Mr. Fox's advice. Years later, he was able to tell Mr. Fox that not only did his business flourish, but the other business also succeeded.

   • Were you surprised at the outcome of the story?

   • Why or why not?

11. To quote Corrie Ten Boom, "When worry and fear are on the throne, you are not an open channel for streams of living water. It is impossible to listen to the Lord's voice while listening to your own fear."

    • How does that statement relate to the author telling us that "once we are convicted of His love for us, and believe that He has a plan for our lives, we have no further need for fear. It becomes irrelevant in our lives, and we see it as the sad and pathetic thief it is"?

12. How do you get to the place where fear no longer exists?

13. Has the study of this book changed your perspective on fear?

    • In what way?

POINTS FOR REVIEW:

▸ When you fear God, you fear nothing else.

▸ When we understand the powerful consequences of our willingness to surrender completely to God, we free ourselves of the world's power to cause us anxiety.

▸ Persist until you succeed.

ABOUT THE AUTHOR

G ary L. Richardson is a nationally recognized trial attorney who has earned a reputation as a hard-fighting courtroom competitor and a powerful negotiator. The embodiment of what it means to live by faith and not by fear, he is passionate about teaching people the truth, the whole truth and nothing but the truth about the destructive power of fear in their lives.

A 1963 graduate of Bethany Nazarene College (now Southern Nazarene University) in Bethany, Oklahoma, Richardson first built a successful career in insurance, and eventually served for two years as assistant insurance commissioner for the state of Oklahoma.

He graduated from South Texas College of Law in Houston in 1972. Licensed in Oklahoma, Texas, and Colorado, Richardson has practiced law since 1974. In addition to his private law practice, Richardson served two years as assistant district attorney in Muskogee County, Oklahoma, and four years as the United States Attorney for the eastern district of Oklahoma (1981-1984).

A member of the Oklahoma Trial Lawyers Association, the Oklahoma and Texas State Bars, the United States Supreme Court, and all United States Federal Courts in Texas and Oklahoma, Richardson also serves on the board of the National Association of Former United States Attorneys. He has been listed in numerous publications as a top trial lawyer — and for ten years straight in the prestigious publication, *The Best Trial Lawyers in America.*

While serving as United States Attorney in the Eastern District of Oklahoma, FBI agents dubbed him the "Smiling Surgeon" because of his skill in cross-examining hostile witnesses and his mild-mannered demeanor in the courtroom while skillfully dissecting a witness's testimony and cutting straight to the heart of the case.

He has won jury verdicts for his clients that set records for the largest awards in eleven different counties in Texas and Oklahoma. He won what is believed to be the largest verdict ever given in Oklahoma for wrongful termination. He is also credited with winning the largest slander jury verdict ever awarded in United States history.

Today, Richardson is known as a crusader against corruption. With a practice limited almost exclusively to representing plaintiffs in civil cases, and an occasional white-collar federal criminal case, Richardson always represents the "little guy" against the "power structure."

I f you liked this book and are interested in others by Gary Richardson, watch the Hensley Publishing website for *Thank God They Ate the Apple!*, and *Bold as a Lion, Harmless as a Lamb*, which will complete a trilogy on how to live fearlessly in unconstrained boldness.

WE WANT TO KNOW WHAT YOU THINK ABOUT THIS BOOK!

Please share your comments about this book by posting your review on our website. From the menu bar at the top of the Hensley Publishing home page, select Bible Studies. On the Bible Studies page, scroll down until you see the cover of this book. (They are listed in alphabetical order.) Choose the book by clicking on the cover image. On the next screen, select **Write a Review**. Write your review and **submit** it.

You can see our complete line of Bible studies, post a review, or order online and save at:

www.hensleypublishing.com

HENSLEY
PUBLISHING
6116 E. 32nd St.
Tulsa, OK 74135